FRENCH REGIONAL COOKERY
BRITTANY

FRENCH REGIONAL COOKERY

BRITTANY

Michael Raffael

HAMLYN

Series consultant MARIE-PIERRE MOINE, editor of
TASTE magazine

Project Editor Camilla Simmons
Art Editor Lisa Tai
Editor Anne Johnson
Designer Mike Leaman
Picture Researcher Gale Carlill
Production Controllers Mandy Inness, Helen Seccombe

Copy editing Jenni Fleetwood
Special Photography Clive Streeter
Food Preparation Eve Dowling, Linda Fraser,
Nichola Palmer, Lyn Rutherford
Styling Marion Price

The publishers would like to thank the following for their
kind permission to reproduce the following photographs:
The Image Bank: pages 6-7; Nick Birch: page 8

Half-title page picture: Galettes au Jambon de Pays; title
page picture: Crabe Pen'march

First published in 1990 by The Hamlyn Publishing Group
Limited
a division of the Octopus Publishing Group
Michelin House
81 Fulham Road
London SW3 6RB

ISBN 0 600 56733 8

Produced by Mandarin Offset

Printed in Hong Kong

CONTENTS

INTRODUCTION

Brittany sticks out of the French hexagon like a wrinkled tongue. It has its own culture, its own language – a close relation of the Celtic Welsh – its own identity and, of course, its own cuisine.

For centuries, the Breton hinterland was among France's poorest provinces. Peasants scraped a living on a staple of buckwheat. Over half their diet was in the form of cereals. Only those with no land went to sea as fishermen.

But the last century has brought about a revolution. Shellfish and crustaceans, turbot, sole and red mullet have become both highly prized and highly priced. Modern methods have transformed Breton agriculture. Tourism has brought the curious in search of typical regional specialities and entrepreneurial restaurateurs have supplied them.

Many gourmets pretend that Brittany does not have its own cooking style. Others go to the other extreme and argue it to be the proud possessor of several hundred authentic recipes. Neither viewpoint is wholly credible. The numbers of genuine dishes found nowhere else are plentiful, but not countless. On the other hand many so-called Breton recipes either have their equivalents in neighbouring regions or are adaptations from the classical repertoire of French cuisine.

To take just one example, consider *homard à l'armoricaine*. There are those who pretend that it is of Breton origin. After all, Armorica is Latin for Brittany and Ar-mor in Celt means seacoast. Most gastronomical authorities, however, will counterclaim that the dish is a bastard form of *homard à l'américaine*, a classic lobster dish fashionable in the mid-nineteenth century. It could not possibly be Breton, they say, because one of the main ingredients, tomatoes, was not even grown in the region at the time. Whatever the rights and wrongs of the debate, Bretons, not too fussed about etymology, have adopted the *à l'armoricaine* version as their own.

Brittany divides conveniently into Ar-mor, the coastline, and Ar-goat (woodland in the literal sense), which is the interior. It is composed of five separate departments. Côtes du Nord faces the Channel. Finistère beside it curls around the tip of the province. Morbihan, next door, has a purely

Atlantic seaboard. Loire-Atlantique, further south, takes its name from France's longest river, which enters the sea beyond Nantes. And Ile-et-Vilaine, where the province's capital Rennes is located, is almost entirely land-locked.

Of the departments, Finistère is the seafood lover's paradise – or would be if overfishing had not made such inroads into the native stock. In ports like Douarnenez, Concarneau and Audierne, there are markets where stalls literally overflow with a crackling, wriggling mass of live prawns, langoustines and assorted crabs. In the docks, fish is sold *à la criée*, which means at auction. The small fish left over is shared among the crews as a kind of tip; it's known as the *godaille* (guzzle) and is turned into a substantial fish soup.

This dish is first cousin of another unique Breton

fish stew, *cotriade*. Every port, every cook has a patent version, but mackerel seems to figure in all of them. There is only one pre-requisite: the fish should be perfectly fresh. It does not come from deep in the holds of trawlers that have been at sea for weeks, but from the inshore fishing fleet which goes out on the tide and returns the same day.

The river Belon in southern Finistère has given its name to the flat oyster which French gourmets admire the most. But the main centre for ostreiculture is in the Gulf of Morbihan at the mouth of the river Auray. In France, oysters are calibrated according to their size; 00 are the largest and number 6 the smallest, though not necessarily less good to eat. Disease has ravaged many oyster beds and several of the cultivators have been forced to import virus-resistant strains of Japanese oyster.

Above Thatched farmhouses and apple orchards are very much part of the Breton landscape, although the apples are more likely to be for pressing than eating, such is the Breton love of cider

Les huîtres are a central part of the *plateau de fruits de mer* – the seafood platter. It's a princely collation of crustaceans and molluscs: clams, winkles, mussels, oysters, cockles, sea urchins, prawns, shrimps, langoustines, crab and lobster. Arranged on a bed of crushed ice and garnished with seaweed, it's the centrepiece of many seaside restaurants.

For seasoning, Bretons prefer sea salt (the best comes from Guérande), because its faint iodine tang adds flavour to a dish as well as saltiness. Salt plays an important role in two other characteristic specialities: in the butter, where man does the adding; and in the *mouton de pré salé,* the lamb nurtured on salt marshes. It's the basic raw material for *gigot à la bretonne,* roast leg of lamb with haricot beans.

Breton butter vies for pride of place with that of Charentes and Normandy. It is the *sine qua non* of the famous fish sauce, *beurre blanc:* high in cholesterol, no doubt, but one of the great French sauces. It's prepared by reducing wine and vinegar with diced shallots and then, over the heat, beating in knobs of butter to form a light creamy texture. An unrefined farmhouse butter gives a far better result because the impurities in it help to stabilize the sauce and prevent it from oiling. Around Nantes, they sometimes add a spoonful of cream and the sauce is turned into *beurre nantais.* Although it is common to find *beurre blanc* served with any fish, it was originally invented to accompany shad, pike, trout and salmon, which thread their way up the Loire and other coastal rivers.

No account of Brittany's gastronomic contribution should overlook the importance of vegetables. The Breton artichoke is larger, rounder and more compacted than other varieties. Cauliflowers tend to reach almost indecent proportions. Thanks to the clement climate brought by the Gulf Stream, spring vegetables – cabbage, beets, potatoes, carrots, turnips and leeks – flow from the region into the giant entrepots of the Paris market, Rungis. To some extent this abundance is the result of modern agro-industrial production, but as much is due to the rich soil around Morlaix in north Finistère.

Bretons are not great lovers of cheese, which they dismiss as 'rotten butter'. But they use cream and other dairy produce almost as much as their Norman neighbours, especially in sauces. *Lait ribot* – buttermilk – is, or was until recently, drunk as the traditional accompaniment to pancakes.

Which leads us to *crêpes* and *galettes,* the province's major contribution to fast food. Every town has at least one crêperie where you will find cooks spreading an even layer of batter on a circular cast-iron griddle, using a tool like a croupier's rake called a *raclette.* Nowadays, most *crêpes* are made with plain flour, but the *galette de sarrasin,* made with buckwheat flour, is still popular, particularly with savouries. The dark flecked flour has so much taste and texture that it is advisable to cut it with a proportion of wholemeal or plain flour.

The range of fillings is virtually endless. *Crêpes aux fruits de mer* is a luxurious dish. There is nothing grand about *galettes* filled with an egg, grated cheese or a sausage, but they are quite delicious. Sweet pancakes may be filled with fruit, drenched in liqueur and flamed, or served with jam, honey or a sweetened *crème de marrons.*

While we're on the subject, the small town of Redon in Ile-et-Vilaine is celebrated for its chestnuts. Every year it holds a fair in their honour when local bakeries compete with each other to create the best chestnut-flavoured gâteaux. Marquees go up in the market place and the Redonnais gather to consume roasted chestnuts and vast quantities of cider.

The pig has pride of place in the farmyard. Country hams, sausages, garlic sausage, andouillette (tripe sausage) and pâtés are all made to secret recipes by village butchers and *charcutiers.* The old saw that everything bar the grunt gets eaten holds true. There are recipes for trotters, tails, ears and the head.

Except along the Loire, cider is the time-honoured alcoholic beverage. It is so much part of the local culture that eating apples are rarely given a place to grow. In the farmhouses, they still press cider apples to brew a rough drink equivalent to English scrumpy. The better ciders are bottled and left to undergo a second fermentation which gives them a sparkling quality. *Cidre brut,* the driest, goes best with shellfish and other seafood; *cidre sec* with pork and poultry; and *cidre doux* with desserts and *crêpes.* Some cider is distilled to make an *eau-de-vie* called Lambig, which is similar to the Calvados of Normandy fame.

The only noteworthy wines come from the southern borders of Brittany around Nantes. Gros plant is a simple, quaffable wine ideal for making fish sauces and, at its best, a worthy accompaniment to seafood. Muscadet, the other regional wine, is prolific but a relative newcomer to the province. The first vineyards were planted in 1737 – whereas cider goes back to at least the fifth century. Made from the *melon* grape, an import from Burgundy where it has never been highly rated, it produces a dry, none-too-acid wine perfect to drink with seafood. It has two slightly different styles. East of Nantes, the Muscadet from the Côteaux de la Loire is stronger and more acidic; south of Nantes in Sèvre-et-Maine, it is more fruity and drunk younger. Some of the better quality Muscadet is bottled from the cask without being filtered. It can have a pleasant touch of sparkle to it and is labelled Muscadet sur lie.

Right: *The day's catch is sorted and packed.*
Brittany enjoys an abundance of seafood and fishing remains an integral part of Breton life

SOUPS

With the sea so much a part of Breton life, many local soups inevitably feature fish or seafood. There is the chowder-like *Soupe Des Jaguins*, for instance, or *Godaille*, made from the small fish left over after the main catch is sold. Other soups tend to be smooth and creamy, like *Soupe de Marrons*, the product of another Breton speciality – chestnuts.

GODAILLE
GUZZLERS' SOUP

SERVES 4
25 g (1 oz) butter
65 g (2½ oz) onion, peeled and finely diced
25 g (1 oz) carrot, peeled and finely diced
15 g (½ oz) celery, finely diced
2 cloves garlic, peeled and crushed
225 g (8 oz) tomatoes, chopped
150 g (5 oz) small fish such as whitebait or sprats
225 g (8 oz) huss
200 ml (⅓ pint) dry Breton or Normandy cider
750 ml (1¼ pints) water
1 bouquet garni
1 pinch of saffron
2 tablespoons cider or white wine vinegar
sea salt and cayenne pepper
TO GARNISH:
2 slices bread
40 g (1½ oz) butter
1 clove garlic, peeled

1 Melt the butter in a large saucepan. Add the onion, carrot and celery. Cook over a gentle heat until tender.

2 Add the garlic, tomatoes, fish, cider and water. Bring to the boil. Add the bouquet garni and saffron. Simmer very gently for 1½ hours. Remove the bouquet garni.

3 Meanwhile, fry the bread in butter. Rub it on both sides with garlic and cut into small cubes.

4 Liquidize the soup, if wished. Stir in the vinegar, season, and return to the boil. Serve with croûtons.

SOUPE DE MOULES SAFRANÉE
MUSSEL SOUP WITH SAFFRON

SERVES 4
2 sachets saffron
200 ml (⅓ pint) milk
150 g (5 oz) butter
100 g (4 oz) shallots, peeled and finely diced
200 ml (⅓ pint) dry white wine, *gros plant*
1 kg (2 lb) mussels, scrubbed and washed
50 g (2 oz) plain flour
900 ml (1½ pints) fish stock
250 ml (8 fl oz) double cream
salt and pepper
2 tablespoons fennel, chopped

1 Boil the milk, add the saffron, and allow to infuse.

2 Melt 50 g (2 oz) butter in a large shallow pan. Add the shallots and stew over a low heat until tender. Pour over the wine and bring to the boil. Add the mussels, cover and cook for about 4 minutes until they open. (Discard any mussels that don't open.)

3 Melt the rest of the butter in a saucepan. Stir in the flour and cook the roux to a sandy texture. Pour the fish stock on to the roux and bring to the boil, stirring continuously. Simmer for 20 minutes.

4 Add the saffron and milk to the thickened stock. Add the cooking liquor from the mussels. Simmer for 10 minutes.

5 Remove the mussels from their shells and add them to the soup. Stir in the cream, season to taste, and, finally, add the fennel. Return to the boil and serve at once.

GODAILLE

SOUPE DES JAGUINS

SOUPE DES JAGUINS
MUSSEL CHOWDER

SERVES 4
75 g (3 oz) salted butter
50 g (2 oz) shallots, peeled and finely diced
100 ml (3½ fl oz) dry white wine, *gros plant*
450 g (1 lb) mussels, scrubbed and washed
120 g (4½ oz) onion, peeled and finely sliced
40 g (1½ oz) plain flour
350 ml (12 fl oz) milk
350 ml (12 fl oz) fish stock
250 g (9 oz) new potatoes, peeled and roughly
chopped
120 ml (4 fl oz) double cream
2 tablespoons chopped parsley
salt and pepper
8 slices French bread, toasted

1 Melt 25 g (1 oz) butter in a large shallow pan. Add the shallots and stew over a low heat until tender. Pour over the wine and bring to the boil. Add the mussels, cover and cook for about 4 minutes until they open. (Discard any mussels that don't open.)

2 Melt the rest of the butter in a saucepan. Add the onion and cook over a low heat until transparent: do not allow to brown. Stir in the flour, add the milk and stock and bring to the boil, stirring to prevent the formation of lumps. Add the cooking liquor from the mussels and the potatoes. Simmer for 20 minutes or until the potatoes are tender.

3 Remove the mussels from their shells and add them to the soup. Stir in the cream and parsley. Season with salt and pepper and serve with toasted French bread.

SOUPE AU CONGRE
CONGER EEL SOUP

SERVES 4 TO 6
1 litre (1¾ pints) water
1 tablespoon dry white wine
2 teaspoons salt
450 g (1 lb) conger eel
250 g (9 oz) onion, peeled and sliced
200 g (7 oz) green cabbage, chopped
100 g (4 oz) frozen peas
300 ml (½ pint) milk
2 tablespoons cornflour
65 g (2½ oz) butter

1 Bring the water, wine and salt to the boil in a large pan. Reduce the heat, add the conger, cover and simmer gently for 30 minutes until the fish is tender. Remove the conger and allow to cool slightly.

2 Add the onion to the broth and simmer for 20 minutes. Add the cabbage and simmer for 10 minutes more. Add the frozen peas and simmer for 2 to 3 minutes.

3 Peel the skin off the conger, fillet it, dice it and remove the bones which you find in the flesh. Add the diced fish to the soup.

4 Heat the milk. Dissolve the cornflour in half a cup of water, stirring until the paste is completely smooth and free of lumps. Whisk the cornflour mixture into the milk and bring to the boil. Whisk the thickened milk into the soup, beat in the butter and serve.

SOUPE DE MARRONS
CHESTNUT SOUP

SERVES 4
50 g (2 oz) butter
65 g (2½ oz) onion, peeled and diced
175 g (6 oz) leek, diced
750 ml (1¼ pints) chicken stock
225 g (8 oz) chestnuts, shelled
100 ml (3½ fl oz) double cream
salt and pepper

1 Melt the butter in a large saucepan. Add the onion and leek. Cover the pan and stew over a low heat for 5 minutes.

2 Pour over the stock, bring to the boil and add the chestnuts. Simmer for 1 hour.

3 Liquidize the soup to form a smooth purée. Return to the pan and add the double cream. Season to taste with salt and pepper and serve.

VELOUTÉ AUX ARTICHAUTS
ARTICHOKE SOUP

SERVES 4
1 litre (1¾ pints) water
2 tablespoons lemon juice
2 large Breton artichokes
65 g (2½ oz) butter
50 g (2 oz) plain flour
400 ml (14 fl oz) chicken stock
120 ml (4 fl oz) double cream
salt and pepper

1 Bring the water and lemon juice to the boil.

2 Break off the artichoke stalks and discard any discoloured or tough outer leaves. Drop the artichokes into the boiling water. Cover and simmer for 30 minutes. Drain and reserve the cooking liquid.

3 Peel away the artichoke leaves and discard the furry choke in the centre. Dice the hearts and reserve as a garnish.

4 Melt the butter in a saucepan and stir in the flour. Cook over gentle heat, stirring continuously, until the roux is golden and forms a sandy texture. Gradually stir in 500 ml (18 fl oz) of the cooking liquid from the artichokes and add the chicken stock. Simmer for 30 minutes. Add the cream and season to taste with salt and pepper. Stir in the diced artichoke hearts just before serving.

LA MITONNÉE
CREAMY ONION SOUP

SERVES 4
300 g (11 oz) onion, peeled and sliced
600 ml (1 pint) milk
250 ml (8 fl oz) chicken stock
1 clove
100 g (4 oz) white bread, cubed
salt and pepper
65 g (2½ oz) butter

1 Put the onion, milk, chicken stock, clove and white bread in a pan with a tight-fitting lid. Simmer very gently for 2½ hours. Check the soup every now and then to see if it is reducing too fast; if necessary, top up with water, and continue cooking until the onion is very soft and the bread has dissolved.

2 Season to taste with salt and pepper and remove the clove. Liquidize the soup. Return it to the pan and beat in the butter just before serving.

LA MITONÉE *(ABOVE)*
VELOUTÉ AUX ARTICHAUTS *BELOW)*

SOUPE DE MORUE *(ABOVE)*
POTAGE DES NANTAIS BRETONS *(BELOW)*

SOUPE DE MORUE
SALT COD SOUP

SERVES 4 TO 6

1.5 kg (3 lb) salt cod, with the head and tail
50 g (2 oz) butter
2 onions, peeled and finely diced
2 cloves garlic, peeled and crushed
575 g (1¼ lb) tomatoes, peeled and chopped
1 litre (1¾ pints) water
120 ml (4 fl oz) dry white wine
1 bay leaf
1 sprig rosemary
1 sprig fennel
1 pinch of saffron
salt and cayenne pepper
400 g (14 oz) potatoes, peeled and chopped

1 Put the salt cod on a rack in a bowl and cover with water. Change the water several times over the next 48 hours to remove the salt. Then peel off the skin.

2 Melt the butter in a large pan and sweat the onions, garlic and tomatoes.

3 Poach the cod in the water for 8 minutes. Pour the water over the onions and tomato. Flake the cod, discarding the head, tail and all the bones, and reserve.

4 Add the wine to the pan and bring to the boil. Add the herbs, saffron, salt and cayenne pepper. Simmer for 30 minutes. Add the potatoes and cook until tender but not disintegrating. Remove the herbs. Stir the cod into the soup and serve.

POTAGE DES NANTAIS BRETONS
HARICOT BEAN SOUP

SERVES 4

250 g (9 oz) haricot beans, soaked overnight
65 g (2½ oz) onion, peeled and chopped
50 g (2 oz) leek, chopped
50 g (2 oz) carrot, peeled and chopped
25 g (1 oz) celery
175 g (6 oz) green streaky bacon in one piece
750 ml (1¼ pints) water
1 bouquet garni
2 tablespoons chopped parsley
salt and pepper
100 g (4 oz) Breton garlic sausage, diced, to garnish

1 Place the beans in a pan with plenty of cold water. Bring to the boil, then reduce the heat and simmer for 1 hour.

2 Drain the beans and transfer to a clean pan with the onion, leek, carrot, celery and bacon. Pour over the water, bring to the boil and add the bouquet garni. Simmer for 2½ hours.

3 Remove the bouquet garni and discard. Remove the piece of bacon and allow to cool slightly. When the bacon is cool enough to handle, pare away and discard the rind, and chop the meat finely.

4 Liquidize the soup and return to the pan. Add the bacon, parsley, and salt and pepper to taste. Bring back to the boil.

5 Add the garnish of diced sausage just before serving. Do not allow it to cook in the soup or it will toughen.

POTAGE MALOUIN
CAULIFLOWER AND POTATO SOUP

SERVES 4
1 small cauliflower weighing about 400 g (14 oz)
25 g (1 oz) butter
25 g (1 oz) onion, peeled and diced
25 g (1 oz) leek, diced
15 g (½ oz) celery, diced
½ bay leaf
1 sprig thyme
750 ml (1¼ pints) chicken stock
75 g (3 oz) potato, peeled and diced
200 ml (⅓ pint) double cream
salt and pepper
2 tablespoons chopped chives to garnish

1 Blanch the cauliflower in boiling water for 10 minutes and drain.

2 Melt the butter in a pan, add the onion, leek, celery and herbs and cook until tender over a low heat. Pour over the stock and bring to the boil. Add the cauliflower and potato. Simmer for 15 minutes. Remove the bay leaf.

3 Liquidize the soup and return to the pan. Add the cream, salt and pepper. Gently heat the soup, but do not allow it to boil or the cream may curdle. Serve at once, garnished with chives.

POTAGE À L'OSEILLE
CREAM OF SORREL SOUP

SERVES 4
400 g (14 oz) sorrel
25 g (1 oz) butter
100 g (4 oz) onion, peeled and diced
1 teaspoon sugar
600 ml (1 pint) chicken stock
100 g (4 oz) potato, peeled and diced
120 ml (4 fl oz) double cream, plus extra to garnish (optional)
salt and pepper
chopped parsley on chervil, to garnish

1 Put the sorrel in a pan with a cup of water. Bring to the boil and cook for about 4 minutes until the sorrel has softened. Drain it over a sieve and squeeze to remove all the moisture.

2 Melt the butter in a pan. Add the onion and stew over a low heat until soft. Add the sugar and stir until dissolved. Pour over the stock and add the sorrel and potato. Bring to the boil, reduce the heat and simmer for 15 minutes.

3 Liquidize the soup. Add the cream and season to taste with salt and pepper. Return to the boil and serve, garnished with chopped parsley or chervil. If wished, a little cream may also be poured over the top of each individual serving, as an extra garnish.

POTAGE À L'OSEILLE

SEAFOOD

Crab, mussels, prawns, oysters – what other food could be more evocative of the sea than these delectable *fruits de mer*? Brittany, with its strong associations with the sea, has many such dishes to offer. Essentially very simply cooked, they are transformed into something truly special with the addition of, say, a herb mayonnaise or a wine and cream sauce. Plainly boiled prawns may be flamed in Calvados, for instance, mussels simmered in Muscadet and tarragon, or lobster enriched with a tomato and wine sauce to create *Homard à l'Amoricaine*.

CRABE À LA MALOUINE
CRAB WITH HERB MAYONNAISE

SERVES 4
1 live cock (male) crab weighing about 1 kg (2 lb)
salt
6 tablespoons mayonnaise
1 teaspoon finely chopped dill
1 teaspoon finely chopped chervil
1 teaspoon finely chopped chives
1 teaspoon finely chopped parsley

1 Place the crab in a large pot of cold salted water (1 heaped teaspoon per 600 ml/1 pint). Cover, bring to the boil and simmer for 10 minutes. Take the crab out of the water and allow to cool. Break off the claws and legs, lever the body out of the shell and discard the stomach sac just behind the eyes.

2 Pick the white meat out of the body, claws and legs. (The French do not use the brown meat – use this to make sandwiches.)

3 Wash the inside of the shell and dry thoroughly. Combine the mayonnaise and herbs and fold in the crabmeat. Spoon the mixture into the shell and serve.

CRABE PEN'MARCH
CRAB WITH PEPPERS AND MINT

SERVES 4
1 live cock (male) crab weighing about 1 kg (2 lb)
salt
6 tablespoons mayonnaise
25 g (1 oz) red capsicum
3 mint leaves, finely chopped
1 chilli, seeded and diced
cucumber slices to garnish

1 Put the crab in a large pot of cold salted water (1 heaped teaspoon per 600 ml/1 pint). Cover, bring to the boil and simmer for 10 minutes. Take the crab out of the water and allow to cool. Break off the claws and legs, lever the body out of the shell, and discard the stomach sac just behind the eyes.

2 Pick the white meat out of the body, claws and legs. (The French do not use the brown meat, use this to make sandwiches).

3 Wash the inside of the shell thoroughly and pat dry. Combine the crabmeat with the mayonnaise, capsicum, mint and chilli. Spoon the mixture into the shell and garnish with cucumber slices.

CRABE PEN'MARCH

CRÊPES AUX FRUITS DE MER

CRÊPES AUX FRUITS DE MER
SHELLFISH PANCAKES

MAKES 8
PANCAKES:
100 g (4 oz) plain flour
1 pinch of salt
300 ml (½ pint) milk
1 egg
1 tablespoon oil
butter
SAUCE:
25 g (1 oz) butter
50 g (2 oz) shallots, peeled and finely diced
1 clove garlic, peeled and crushed
150 g (5 oz) tomatoes, peeled, seeded and chopped
6 tablespoons fish stock
1 tablespoon dry cider
120 ml (4 fl oz) double cream
salt and pepper
FILLING:
16 cooked mussels
1 cooked lobster tail, sliced
100 g (4 oz) shelled prawns
4 scallops, sliced

1 First make a pancake batter. Sift the flour and salt into a bowl. Beat in the milk and egg, and finally stir in the oil. Allow to rest for 1 hour. Heat a little butter in a 20 cm (8 inch) frying pan. Make eight pancakes and keep hot.

2 Melt the butter for the sauce in another pan. Sauté the shallots. Add the garlic and tomatoes and cook until soft. Pour over the fish stock and cider. Reduce to a glaze, then add the cream and heat to a light coating consistency. Season with salt and pepper.

3 Add all the shellfish to the sauce away from the heat and leave for 2 or 3 minutes to heat through. Spoon the filling on to the pancakes, roll up and serve.

LANGOUSTE GRILLÉE AUX HERBES
GRILLED CRAWFISH WITH HERBS

SERVES 4
salt and pepper
1 crawfish weighing about 1.75 kg (4 lb)
50 g (2 oz) butter, melted
1 tablespoon Calvados
SAUCE:
40 g (1½ oz) shallots, peeled and finely diced
4 tablespoons Muscadet
4 tablespoons white wine vinegar
salt and pepper
150 g (5 oz) butter
1 sprig fennel leaves, roughly chopped
1 sprig chervil leaves, roughly chopped
1 sprig parsley, roughly chopped

1 Bring a large pan of water to the boil. Add salt at the rate of 10 g per litre (1 teaspoon per pint). Drop the crawfish head-first into the boiling water and cook for 15 minutes. Drain, cool and split lengthwise.

2 Brush the crawfish halves with 25 g (1 oz) butter. Grill for 6 minutes, turning once. Brush with the remaining butter and grill for another 6 minutes. Flame with Calvados and season with salt and pepper.

3 Put the shallots, wine and vinegar in a pan and reduce to a glaze. Season with salt and pepper and whisk in the butter. Spoon a little sauce over the crawfish, garnish with herbs, and hand the rest of the sauce separately.

GRATIN DE MOULES
GRATINÉED MUSSELS

SERVES 4
THE BUTTER:
40 g (1½ oz) shallots, finely diced
3 cloves garlic, peeled and crushed
3 tablespoons chopped parsley
250 g (9 oz) salted butter, softened
THE MUSSELS:
50 g (2 oz) salted butter
100 g (4 oz) shallots, peeled and finely diced
100 ml (3½ fl oz) dry white wine, *gros plant*
48 large mussels, scrubbed and washed
1 teaspoon curry powder
50 g (2 oz) dry or toasted breadcrumbs

1 First prepare the butter. Combine the shallots, garlic, parsley and softened butter, so that they form a smooth, well-blended mixture.

2 Then prepare the mussels. Melt the butter in a large, shallow pan. Add the shallots and stew over a low heat until tender. Pour over the wine and bring to the boil. Add the mussels, cover and cook for about 4 minutes until they open. (Discard any that do not open.) Allow to cool and drain. Discard half the shells, leaving the mussels attached to the remaining halves.

3 Spread a little butter mixture over each mussel. Sprinkle with a hint of curry powder and coat with an even layer of breadcrumbs.

4 Put the mussels in four gratin dishes and bake in a hot oven, at 230°C (450°F), Gas mark 8, for 8 to 10 minutes until golden brown.

MOULES GLACÉES
GLAZED MUSSELS

SERVES 4
175 g (6 oz) unsalted butter
100 g (4 oz) shallots, peeled and finely diced
1 clove garlic, peeled and crushed
2 teaspoons dried tarragon
200 ml (⅓ pint) Muscadet
48 large mussels, scrubbed and washed
3 egg yolks
2 tablespoons chopped chives

1 Melt 50 g (2 oz) butter in a large shallow pan. Add the shallots, garlic and tarragon. Stew over a low heat until the shallots are soft. Pour over the wine and bring to the boil. Add the mussels, cover and cook for about 4 minutes until they open, shaking them well, then remove from the pan. (You may have to do this in two batches.) Discard any mussels that don't open.

2 Reduce the mussel liquor to a glaze. Transfer this to a heat-resistant bowl and stand it over a pan of simmering water. Beat in the egg yolks until they are well amalgamated with the shallots, then whisk in the remaining butter, a few pieces at a time, so as to obtain a creamy emulsified sauce. Add the chives.

3 Discard one half of each mussel shell and spoon a teaspoon of sauce over each mussel, still in the other half shell. Glaze in a very hot oven, at 240°C (475°F), Gas Mark 9, for 2 to 3 minutes. Arrange immediately on four plates, 12 per plate.

Moules glacées *(ABOVE)*
COQUILLES SAINT-JACQUES ROTIES AU FOUR *(BELOW, RECIPE PAGE 26)*

COQUILLES SAINT-JACQUES RÔTIES AU FOUR
BAKED SCALLOPS

SERVES 4

8 scallops on their shells (you will need 4 curved and 4 flat shells)
120 g (4½ oz) butter, softened
12 basil leaves, torn into pieces
1 teaspoon chopped parsley
1 teaspoon chopped chervil
salt and pepper
250 g (9 oz) plain flour

1 Remove the scallops from their shells; wash the shells and reserve. Arrange the scallops in the four curved shells, along with the butter, torn basil leaves and chopped herbs. Season with salt and pepper.

2 Mix the flour with enough water to make a malleable paste. Divide into four and roll into thin strips. Lay them around the outside edges of the four filled scallop shells. Press four flat shells on top, using the flour paste as a seal and making sure that the edges of the shells are tightly closed together.

3 Bake the scallops in a hot oven, at 220°C (425°F), Gas Mark 7, for 8 to 10 minutes. Open the shells by breaking the pastry seal and prising away the top shell. Serve the scallops at once, in their shells.

CREVETTES FLAMBÉES
FLAMED PRAWNS

SERVES 4

salt
48 large, fresh prawns
6 tablespoons sunflower or groundnut oil
6 tablespoons Lambig (or Calvados)

1 Bring a large pan of water to the boil. Add about 10 g salt per litre (1 teaspoon per pint). Drop half the prawns into the water. Boil for 3 minutes and drain. Repeat the process with the remaining prawns.

2 Heat the oil until nearly smoking in a large flameproof pan. Add the prawns and stir until they are well coated in oil. Pour over half the Lambig or Calvados and flame. When the flames start to die down, add the remaining spirit and bring the prawns, still flaming, to the table.

HOMARD À LA NAGE
POACHED LOBSTER

SERVES 4

2 live lobsters, each weighing 575 g (1¼ lb)
75 g (3 oz) butter, melted
COURT-BOUILLON:
3 litres (5½ pints) water
120 ml (4 fl oz) dry white wine
1 tablespoon white wine vinegar
25 g (1 oz) salt
15 g (½ oz) parsley stalks
1 bunch spring onions, finely chopped
1 bay leaf
6 crushed peppercorns

1 Put all the ingredients for the *court-bouillon* in a large pan. Bring to the boil and simmer for 10 minutes.

2 Grasp 1 lobster firmly around the body (not the tail). Plunge it head-first into the *nage*. Simmer until red all over, remove and repeat with the second lobster.

3 To serve, split the 2 lobsters lengthwise, remove the stomach sacs behind the eyes and crack the claws. Arrange the halves on a serving dish, paint with melted butter and serve the rest of the butter in a sauceboat.

HOMARD À LA NAGE

BROCHETTES DE SAINT-JACQUES *(ABOVE)*
HOMARD À L'ARMORICAINE *(BELOW)*

BROCHETTES DE SAINT-JACQUES
SCALLOP KEBABS

SERVES 4
4 slices smoked streaky bacon
16 scallops
50 g (2 oz) butter
salt and pepper
1 tablespoon Cognac
2 teaspoons tomato purée
1 clove garlic, peeled and crushed
250 ml (8 fl oz) double cream
1 tablespoon chopped dill

1 Remove the rind from the bacon and blanch the rashers in boiling water for 2 minutes. Drain and cut each rasher into five pieces. Thread alternate pieces of bacon and scallops on four skewers, starting and finishing with a piece of bacon.

2 Melt the butter in a large oval pan (large enough to take the skewered scallops). Sauté the scallops in the butter for 4 minutes so that they are lightly coloured on all sides. Season with salt and pepper and drain. Keep hot.

3 Discard any fat in the pan. Flame with Cognac. Add the tomato purée and garlic. Cook for 30 seconds, then add the cream. Heat to a light coating consistency and adjust the seasoning. Stir in the dill. Heat for 10 seconds and spoon the sauce around the *brochettes*.

HOMARD À L'ARMORICAINE
LOBSTER SAUTÉED IN A TOMATO AND BRANDY SAUCE

SERVES 2
1 live hen (female) lobster, with eggs, weighing 750 g (1½ lb)
2 tablespoons sunflower or groundnut oil
50 g (2 oz) butter
1 tablespoon Cognac
2 shallots, peeled and finely diced
½ teaspoon paprika
1 carrot, peeled and finely diced
150 g (5 oz) tomatoes, peeled, seeded and chopped
6 tablespoons fish stock
1 tablespoon dry white wine
1 tablespoon chopped tarragon
salt and pepper

1 Lay the lobster flat in a large serving dish. Hold the point of a cooking knife on the cross in the centre of the shell and bring it down sharply. This kills the lobster at once, though its reflexes may cause it to twitch. Cut off the claws and crack them. Cut off the legs. Split the carcass and remove the stomach sac behind the eyes. Scoop out the soft parts and reserve. Scoop out the eggs from under the tail and reserve. Split the tail and remove the intestine.

2 Heat the oil and half the butter in a large pan. Sauté the lobster pieces until they turn red. Flame with Cognac and remove from the pan.

3 Add the shallots, paprika and carrot to the pan and cook until soft. Add the tomatoes, stock and wine. Return the lobster to the pan and simmer for 15 minutes.

4 Blend the remaining butter with the lobster eggs and the reserved soft parts. (Do this in a food processor or with a mortar and pestle.)

5 Take the lobster pieces from the pan and arrange in a serving dish. Reduce the sauce slightly. Add the tarragon, whisk in the lobster butter, stir until thickened, and season. Pour the sauce over the lobster and serve.

ARAIGNÉE À LA BRETONNE

ARAIGNÉE À LA BRETONNE
SPIDER CRAB WITH PRAWNS AND MUSSELS

SERVES 4
1 large live spider crab
salt
12 cooked mussels
8 prawns, cooked and shelled
1 teaspoon finely chopped chives to garnish
DRESSING:
1 tablespoon lemon juice
½ teaspoon Dijon mustard
1 tablespoon virgin olive oil
2 tablespoons sunflower or groundnut oil
salt and pepper

1 Scrub the spider crab thoroughly to remove traces of mud and sand. Place in a large pot of cold salted water (1 heaped teaspoon per 600 ml/1 pint). Cover, bring to the boil and simmer for 10 minutes. Take the crab out of the water and allow to cool. Break off the legs and claws, lever the body out of the shell, and discard the stomach sac behind the eyes.

2 Pick the white meat out of the body, claws and legs. (Reserve the brown meat for use in sandwiches).

3 In a bowl, combine the dressing ingredients. Fold the crab, mussels and prawns into the dressing. Fill the shell with the mixture and garnish with chives.

HUITRES POCHÉES AU CHAMPAGNE
OYSTERS POACHED IN CHAMPAGNE

SERVES 4
24 flat Belon oysters
200 ml (⅓ pint) brut Champagne
300 ml (½ pint) double cream
salt and cayenne pepper
1 large egg yolk

1 Open the oysters, pouring their juices into a pan. Put the oysters in the pan with their juices and the Champagne. Bring to simmering point, drain and remove the beards. Arrange the oysters in half shells and transfer to a very cool oven, 110°C (225°F), Gas Mark ¼. Leave the oven door open so that they do *not* cook.

2 Reduce the stock by three-quarters. Add the cream. Heat to a light coating consistency. Season and beat in the yolk.

3 Spoon the sauce over the oysters. Glaze under the grill and serve.

LANGOUSTINES AU GROS PLANT
LANGOUSTINES IN A WINE AND CREAM SAUCE

SERVES 4
1 bottle dry white wine, *gros plant*
1 litre (1¾ pints) fish stock
15 g (½ oz) salt
48 langoustines
50 g (2 oz) butter
50 g (2 oz) shallots, peeled and finely diced
250 ml (8 fl oz) double cream
TO GARNISH:
8 baby spring carrots
120 g (4½ oz) French beans
1 courgette, sliced

1 Put the wine, stock and salt in a pan, and simmer for 5 minutes. Drop 6 langoustines into the stock. Simmer for 3 minutes and drain. Repeat with the remaining langoustines, allow to cool, then shell the tails.

2 Melt the butter in a large pan. Cook the shallots over a low heat until soft. Turn up the heat and sauté the langoustine tails for about 2 minutes. Remove them with a slotted spoon and keep hot.

3 Add 250 ml (8 fl oz) stock to the pan and reduce to a glaze. Whisk in the cream and reduce to a coating consistency. Boil the vegetables for the garnish.

4 Adjust the seasoning of the sauce. Return the langoustines to the pan to reheat, then arrange on a serving dish, pour over the sauce and garnish.

FISH

When it comes to fish dishes, the Breton cook is especially fortunate for she can choose from the bounty of either sea or river. The varieties thus available are as numerous as the ways of cooking them. A particular Breton speciality is *Cotriade*, a generous mix of fish chunks simmered in wine. Other fish may be cooked whole and combined with seafood, as in *Dorade à la Brestoise*, or served cold, as in *Maquereaux au Vin Blanc*, while fresh sardines are treated with the simplicity they deserve – plainly grilled and served with lemon.

COTRIADE
BRETON FISH STEW

SERVES 6 TO 8
50 g (2 oz) dripping or bacon fat
250 g (9 oz) onions, peeled and sliced
575 g (1¼ lb) waxy potatoes, peeled and roughly chopped
1.2 litres (2 pints) water
150 ml (¼ pint) dry white wine
3 teapoons salt
4 conger steaks, each weighing 150 g (5 oz)
450 g (1 lb) huss, cut into eight pieces
2 gurnards, cut into steaks (minus the heads)
2 mackerel, cut into steaks (minus the heads)
450 g (1 lb) whiting fillets, cut into eight pieces
VINAIGRETTE:
2 tablespoons white wine vinegar
1 tablespoon finely diced shallots
½ teaspoon mustard
salt and pepper
6 tablespoons olive oil
2 tablespoons chopped parsley

1 Melt the fat in a large pan and sauté the onions until well coloured. Add the potatoes, water and wine and bring to the boil. Season with salt.

2 Add the conger and simmer for 20 minutes. Add the huss, gurnards and mackerel and simmer for another 10 minutes. Finally add the whiting and take the pan off the heat. Adjust the seasoning.

3 Combine the vinegar, shallots, mustard, salt and pepper in a bowl. Beat in the oil and finally the parsley.

4 Carefully remove the fish from the broth together with the potatoes and arrange in a large serving dish. Add two ladles of broth to the fish. Finally spoon over the vinaigrette, so that all the fish is well coated. Serve the broth separately with thick slices of French bread or large croûtons.

AIGLE DE MER AU BEURRE NOISETTE
SKATE WITH BROWN BUTTER

SERVES 4
500 ml (18 fl oz) water
6 tablespoons white wine vinegar
4 skate wings, each weighing 175 g (6 oz)
1 teaspoon salt
1 tablespoon chopped parsley
65 g (2½ oz) butter
1 tablespoon red wine vinegar
4 teaspoons drained capers

1 Bring the water and white wine vinegar to simmering point in a large skillet or sauté pan. Add the skate and salt. Simmer for 10 to 12 minutes. Drain the skate and remove any skin. Pat dry with absorbent paper and keep hot on a serving dish.

2 To serve, sprinkle parsley over the skate. Heat the butter in a pan until it starts to brown and pour over the skate. Deglaze the pan in which the butter was heated with red wine vinegar, add the capers and spoon over the fish. Serve at once. Ideally, the butter should still be hot and sizzling when the dish reaches the table.

COTRIADE

DORADE À LA BRESTOISE

BRANDADE DE THON
CREAMED TUNA FISH

SERVES 4

1 × 200 g (7 oz) can tuna in olive oil
300 g (11 oz) potatoes, peeled
salt
1 clove garlic, peeled and crushed
250 ml (8 fl oz) olive oil
3 tablespoons double cream
40 g (1½ oz) cheese, grated

1 Put the tuna in a bowl and mash with a fork. Boil the potatoes in salted water and mash. Combine with the tuna and add the garlic.

2 Beat the oil into the tuna and potato mixture a little at a time. Fold in the cream and check the seasoning. Spoon the mixture into four ramekins. Sprinkle with grated cheese and bake in a moderately hot oven, at 200°C (400°F) Gas Mark 6, for 10 minutes. Serve with toast or crusty bread.

DORADE À LA BRESTOISE
BRAISED SEA BREAM WITH PRAWNS

SERVES 4

5 tablespoons dry white wine
120 ml (4 fl oz) fish stock
40 g (1½ oz) butter
50 g (2 oz) shallots, peeled and finely diced
2 cloves garlic, peeled and crushed
salt and pepper
1 sea bream weighing about 1 kg (2 lb)
TO GARNISH:
25 g (1 oz) butter
120 g (4½ oz) mushrooms, sliced
100 g (4 oz) shelled prawns
100 g (4 oz) shelled mussels (optional)

1 Place the wine and stock together in a saucepan, and bring to the boil.

2 Brush the bottom of a large ovenproof dish with a little of the butter and place the shallots and garlic on top. Rub salt and pepper on the inside and outside of the bream. Make two cuts in the flesh on one side. Rub with the rest of the butter and lay, cut side up, in the dish. Pour over the wine and stock. Bake in a moderate oven, at 180°C (350°F), Gas mark 4, for 30 minutes, basting once or twice.

3 To prepare the garnish, melt the butter in a pan and sauté the mushrooms. Add the mushrooms, prawns and mussels to the dish and serve.

DARNES DE SAUMON EN PAPILLOTE
SALMON STEAKS BAKED IN FOIL

SERVES 4

1 kg (2 lb) salmon, middle cut
50 g (2 oz) butter, melted
40 g (1½ oz) onion, peeled and finely diced
40 g (1½ oz) celery, cut in *julienne*
40 g (1½ oz) leek, cut in *julienne*
50 g (2 oz) carrot, peeled and cut in *julienne*
1 tablespoon chopped chives
salt and pepper
4 tablespoons Muscadet

1 Scrape the scales off the salmon and wipe clean. Cut into four steaks. Brush four sheets of foil, large enough to wrap the steaks, with butter. Lay the steaks on top.

2 Blanch the onion, celery, leek and carrot in boiling water for 2 minutes. Drain.

3 Sprinkle the blanched vegetables and chopped chives over the salmon and season with salt and pepper. Wrap up the foil parcels and pour the wine into them just before sealing. It should not escape from the foil during cooking. Bake in a moderately hot oven, at 190°C (375°F), Gas Mark 5, for 20 minutes, and serve.

SARDINES GRILLÉES
GRILLED SARDINES

SERVES 4

1 kg (2 lb) sardines
oil
salt and pepper
1 lemon, quartered

1 Do not scale or gut the sardines. Brush with oil and grill. Allow 3 to 4 minutes on each side, depending on the heat of the grill and the size of the sardines. The skins should start to blister and char.

2 Drain the fish on absorbent paper. Season with salt and pepper and serve on a plate garnished with lemon quarters. Sardines should really be eaten with the fingers: pick away the skin, which is rather indigestible, and eat the flesh underneath.

BROCHET AU BEURRE BLANC
PIKE WITH BUTTER SAUCE

SERVES 4

1 pike weighing about 1.5 kg (3½ lb), cleaned
COURT-BOUILLON:
225 g (8 oz) onion, peeled and sliced
120 g (4½ oz) carrot, peeled and finely sliced
15 g (½ oz) parsley stalks
1 sprig thyme
½ bay leaf
1 bottle dry white wine, *gros plant*
1 tablespoon white wine vinegar
1.5 litres (2½ pints) water
25 g (1 oz) salt
1 teaspoon crushed peppercorns
SAUCE:
100 g (4 oz) shallots, peeled and finely diced
6 tablespoons dry white wine
6 tablespoons white wine vinegar
salt and pepper
350 g (12 oz) butter

1 Put all the ingredients for the *court-bouillon* except for the peppercorns in a pan. Simmer for 20 minutes. Add the peppercorns and simmer for another 15 minutes. Strain into a fish kettle roughly the size of the pike.

2 Sprinkle the inside of the pike with salt. Leave for 30 minutes and rinse. Place the fish in the fish kettle. Bring to the boil and simmer for 15 to 20 minutes. Drain the fish, lift off the skin and arrange on a serving dish.

3 To make the sauce, put the shallots, wine, vinegar, salt and pepper in an enamelled pan (not aluminium). Cook until most of the liquid has evaporated. Cut the butter into small pieces and beat into the reduction, a few knobs at a time. Strain the sauce before serving.

MATELOTE DE THON AUX PRUNEAUX
TUNA IN RED WINE WITH PRUNES

SERVES 4

65 g (2½ oz) butter
40 g (1½ oz) green streaky bacon, diced
100 g (4 oz) onion, peeled and sliced
4 tuna steaks, each weighing 175 g (6 oz)
2 cloves garlic, peeled and crushed
1 sprig thyme
1 sprig fennel
4 parsley stalks
400 ml (14 fl oz) red wine
16 prunes, soaked overnight
200 g (7 oz) button mushrooms
salt
40 g (1½ oz) plain flour
freshly ground black pepper

1 Melt 15 g (½ oz) butter in a pan. Add the bacon and fry until lightly coloured. Add the onion, cover and sweat over a low heat until softened.

2 Lay the tuna on top and sprinkle with garlic. Add the herbs, tied in a bunch. Pour over the wine, and simmer for 10 minutes. Add the prunes and mushrooms. Season with salt. Simmer for 15 minutes.

3 Transfer the tuna, prunes and mushrooms to a serving dish and keep hot. Rub the rest of the butter into the flour. Whisk into the sauce and allow to thicken but do not boil. Season with pepper, pour over the fish and serve.

BROCHET AU BEURRE BLANC

NAVARIN DE LOTTE *(ABOVE)*
SALADE QUIMPERLAISE *(BELOW)*

MAQUEREAUX AU VIN BLANC
COLD MACKEREL IN WHITE WINE

SERVES 4
300 ml (½ pint) dry white wine
300 ml (½ pint) water
1 rounded teaspoon salt
1 bay leaf
1 sprig fennel
50 g (2 oz) onion, peeled and finely sliced
½ lemon, sliced
6 black peppercorns
4 mackerel, each weighing 175 g (6 oz)

·1 Put all the ingredients except for the fish into a pan. Simmer for 15 minutes. Add the fish to the liquid and simmer for another 15 minutes. Allow to cool in the liquid.

2 Refrigerate for 24 hours before serving.

NAVARIN DE LOTTE
MONKFISH WITH SPRING VEGETABLES

SERVES 4
65 g (2½ oz) butter
100 g (4 oz) onion, peeled and finely diced
1 clove garlic, peeled and crushed
250 g (9 oz) tomatoes, peeled, seeded and chopped
1 teaspoon tomato purée
5 tablespoons dry white wine
200 ml (⅓ pint) fish stock
1 bouquet garni
6 tablespoons double cream
salt and pepper
750 g (1½ lb) monkfish, cut in 2.5 cm (1 inch) cubes
TO GARNISH:
8 small turnips, peeled and quartered
200 g (7 oz) baby carrots, sliced
white parts of 8 spring onions
100 g (4 oz) frozen peas
salt
2 tablespoons chopped chives

1 Melt 25 g (1 oz) butter in a pan. Add the onion and cook over a moderate heat until soft. Add the garlic, tomatoes, tomato purée, wine, stock and bouquet garni. Simmer very gently for 30 minutes. Pass the mixture through a sieve. Put into a clean pan with the cream. Heat to a coating consistency and season with salt and pepper.

2 Heat the remaining butter in a skillet and sauté the monkfish for about 4 minutes until just cooked.

3 Boil the vegetables for the garnish in salted water, and drain.

4 Drain the monkfish and pat dry. Combine with the sauce and garnish with the vegetables. Sprinkle with the chives.

SALADE QUIMPERLAISE
BRETON FISH SALAD

SERVES 4
1 small cooked lobster
12 shelled prawns
24 shelled mussels
DRESSING:
1 tablespoon finely diced shallots
1 tablespoon cider vinegar
½ teaspoon mustard
2 tablespoons sunflower or groundnut oil
1 tablespoon walnut oil
salt and pepper
SALAD LEAVES:
8 radicchio leaves
8 endive leaves
8 oak leaf lettuce leaves
8 cabbage lettuce leaves
20 sprigs watercress

1 Combine the shallots, vinegar and mustard. Beat in the oils, a little at a time, and season with salt and pepper.

2 Shell and chop the lobster. Toss the shellfish in a third of the dressing.

3 Tear the salad leaves into bite-sized pieces. Combine with the remaining dressing. Arrange with the shellfish on four plates and serve.

SOLE ROSCOFF
SOLE WITH LOBSTER, PAPRIKA, CREAM AND TOMATO SAUCE

SERVES 4
50 g (2 oz) butter
50 g (2 oz) shallots, peeled and diced
1 teaspoon paprika
200 ml (⅓ pint) fish stock
3 tablespoons dry white wine
salt and pepper
4 dover soles, each weighing 350 g (12 oz),
skinned and trimmed
150 g (5 oz) tomatoes, peeled, seeded and diced
TO GARNISH:
1 cooked lobster tail, sliced
a few chervil leaves

1 Melt half the butter in a large skillet. Sweat the shallots over a low heat. Add the paprika and cook for 1 more minute. Pour over the fish stock and wine and bring to the boil. Season lightly with salt and pepper.

2 Place the soles in the skillet and poach for about 8 minutes, turning them after 5 minutes. Remove carefully from the skillet and keep hot on a serving dish.

3 Add the tomatoes to the liquid and reduce by two-thirds by boiling rapidly over a high heat. Beat the rest of the butter into the sauce.

4 Heat the sliced lobster tail in the sauce for a few minutes and remove. Spoon the sauce over the soles. Garnish with the slices of lobster tail and a little chervil.

HARENGS QUIMPERLAISE
FRIED HERRINGS WITH HERB AND MUSTARD SAUCE

SERVES 4
4 large herrings, cleaned and with heads and
tails removed
12 parsley stalks
4 tablespoons olive oil
sea salt and black pepper
SAUCE:
2 egg yolks
2 teaspoons Dijon mustard
2 teaspoons white wine vinegar
90 g (3½ oz) butter, melted
2 tablespoons chopped fresh herbs including
parsley, chives and tarragon
salt and pepper

1 Rinse the herrings and place the parsley stalks inside the fish. Roll the fish in oil and season generously with salt and pepper. Leave for at least 1 hour.

2 Stand a basin over a pan of simmering water. Add the egg yolks, mustard and half the vinegar, and beat for about 1 minute. Whisk in the butter a little at a time to make a smooth emulsified sauce. Whisk in the remaining vinegar. Stir in the herbs, salt and pepper and keep warm.

3 Fry the herrings for 10 to 12 minutes. Turn them after 6 minutes. Serve accompanied by the sauce.

H ARENGS À LA NANTAISE *(ABOVE, RECIPE PAGE 43)*
SOLE ROSCOFF

FILETS DE BARBUE À LA CANOTIÈRE

HARENGS À LA NANTAISE
GRILLED HERRINGS WITH SOFT ROE BUTTER

SERVES 4
4 large herrings, cleaned
oil
pepper
ROE BUTTER:
salt
65 g (2½ oz) soft herring roes
100 g (4 oz) butter, softened
1 heaped teaspoon strong Dijon mustard
TO GARNISH:
slices of lemon
4 sprigs of chervil

1 First make the roe butter. Bring a small pan of salted water to simmering point. Poach the roes for 8 to 10 minutes. Drain and allow to cool.

2 Pound the roes, butter and mustard until smooth. Sieve the roe butter and fill a piping bag with a star tube with the mixture.

3 Brush the herrings with oil. (You may cut off the heads and tails if you prefer.) Grill for 10 to 12 minutes. Season generously with pepper.

4 To serve, lay the herrings on a plate and pipe a whirl of roe butter along one side. Garnish each herring with slices of lemon and a sprig of chervil.

FILETS DE BARBUE À LA CANOTIÈRE
BRILL FILLETS IN MUSCADET AND WILD MUSHROOM SAUCE

SERVES 4
1 brill weighing 1.5 kg (3½ lb)
1 medium onion, peeled and chopped
50 g (2 oz) mushroom trimmings
4 parsley stalks
1 bay leaf
1 sprig thyme
300 ml (½ pint) water
300 ml (½ pint) Muscadet
salt and pepper
200 g (7 oz) oyster mushrooms, sliced
250 ml (8 fl oz) double cream
50 g (2 oz) butter
1 tablespoon chopped chives

1 Fillet the brill and remove the skin. Chop the head and bones into small pieces. Put these in a pan with the skin, onion, mushroom trimmings, parsley stalks, bay leaf and thyme. Pour over the water and wine. Bring to the boil, skim and simmer for 25 minutes. Strain the stock into an enamelled cast iron dish and add a little salt.

2 Lay the fillets of brill and oyster mushrooms in the stock. Bring to simmering point. Cover with a sheet of foil and poach for 5 minutes.

3 Carefully remove the fillets and keep hot. Reduce the liquid by two-thirds. Add the cream. Heat to a light coating consistency and season with salt and pepper. Beat in the butter and add the chopped chives.

4 Spoon the sauce on to four plates and lay the fillets of fish on top.

MEAT AND POULTRY

Pork, lamb, beef, poultry and game are all to be found in Breton cuisine, the *mouton de pré salé* (lamb grazed on salt marshes) being the best known. What sets Breton meat cooking apart from that of other French provinces, however, is its use of the spicy and sweet. In *Kig Ha Farz*, for example, pork and beef is served with slices of dried fruit dumpling, while *Boulettes Bretonnes* are flavoured with nutmeg, cloves and mixed herbs.

GIGOT À LA BRETONNE
ROAST LEG OF LAMB WITH HARICOT BEANS

SERVES 8
250 g (9 oz) haricot beans
2 cloves garlic, peeled
1 leg of lamb, weighing about 2.25 kg (5 lb)
and cut on the round like a ham
salt and pepper
2 medium onions, peeled
1 large carrot, peeled
25 g (1 oz) celery
40 g (1½ oz) butter
3 tomatoes, peeled and chopped
1 teaspoon tomato purée
1 tablespoon chopped chervil
chervil sprigs, to garnish

1 Soak the beans overnight in three times their volume of water. Cut the garlic into slivers and insert at intervals in the lamb. Season the joint with salt and pepper.

2 Put the beans in a pan of fresh water with 1 onion, the carrot and celery. Simmer for 1½ to 3 hours until tender.

3 Put the joint on a rack over a roasting tin. Roast in a very hot oven, at 240°C (475°F), Gas Mark 9, for 10 minutes. Reduce the heat to 190°C (375°F), Gas Mark 5 and roast for a further 25 minutes per kg (2¼ lb). If you have a meat thermometer, the internal temperature should be 65°C (150°F). Rest the joint for 15 minutes before carving.

4 Slice the remaining onion. Fry in butter. Add the tomatoes and tomato purée and cook until tender. Pour in the meat juices. Add the chervil and adjust the seasoning. Drain the beans and cook in the tomato sauce for 5 minutes. Serve the joint surrounded by the beans and garnished with chervil sprigs.

CARRÉ D'AGNEAU AU BEURRE BRETON
BEST END OF LAMB WITH HERB BUTTER

SERVES 4
2 best ends of lamb, each one with 5 ribs
2 cloves garlic, peeled
20 g (¾ oz) butter, melted
salt and pepper
HERB BUTTER:
120 g (4½ oz) butter
1 tablespoon chopped parsley
1 tablespoon chopped chives
1 tablespoon chopped chervil
2 teaspoons chopped tarragon
1 tablespoon finely diced shallots

1 Rub the lamb with garlic and leave for 2 hours. Preheat the oven to 220°C (425°F), Gas Mark 7. Brush the meat with melted butter, season with salt and pepper and roast on a rack over a roasting tin for 20 to 25 minutes. Baste once. Allow the meat to rest for 10 minutes before carving.

2 Meanwhile, prepare the herb butter. Cream the butter. Blanch the herbs and shallots in boiling water for 30 seconds. Drain and press out the moisture. Beat the herbs and shallots into the creamed butter. Serve the butter in a dish as an accompaniment to the meat: it should still be soft.

GIGOT À LA BRETONNE

CANETON BRAISÉ AU MUSCADET

CANETON BRAISÉ AU MUSCADET
DUCK BRAISED IN MUSCADET

SERVES 4
1 duck weighing about 1.75 kg (4 lb)
150 g (5 oz) onion and carrot, peeled and
chopped
1 tablespoon chopped parsley stalks
500 ml (18 fl oz) Muscadet
salt and pepper
500 ml (18 fl oz) double cream
TO GARNISH:
50 g (2 oz) butter
2 apples, peeled, cored and sliced

1 Take the neck and giblets from the duck and chop up finely. Put these in a roasting tin with the onion, carrot and parsley stalks, place the duck on top and roast in a hot oven, at 220°C (425°F), Gas Mark 7, for 30 minutes.

2 Take the duck out of the oven and pour off the fat. Pour over the wine and season with salt and pepper. Turn the oven down to 190°C (375°F), Gas Mark 5, return the duck to the oven and braise for a further 30 minutes.

3 Strain the juices in the tin into a pan and reduce to a glaze over a vigorous heat. (Discard the vegetables or reserve to serve with the duck.) Add the cream and heat to a light coating consistency. Adjust the seasoning.

4 Melt the butter in a pan and fry the apple slices until golden. Serve the duck garnished with apple and serve the sauce in a sauceboat.

JAMBONNETTE DE CANARD NANTAIS
STUFFED DUCK LEGS

SERVES 2
1 duck weighing about 1.75 kg (4 lb)
1 teaspoon crushed green peppercorns
1 shallot, peeled and finely diced
salt
25 g (1 oz) onion, peeled and finely diced
15 g (½ oz) celery, finely diced
15 g (½ oz) carrot, peeled and finely diced
½ teaspoon tomato purée
200 ml (⅓ pint) duck or chicken stock
100 ml (3½ fl oz) Madeira
1 tablespoon raisins
150 ml (¼ pint) double cream

1 Remove the legs from the duck: cut round the line of the thighs, break the bone against the joint and free from the carcass. Then bone out the legs: cut the skin round the end of the drumstick and scrape the meat from around the bones. Pull out the bones. Remove the skin from the duck breast (and use to make Salade à la Peau de Canard, page 59). Chop the breast meat into small pieces. Preheat the oven to 160°C (325°F), Gas Mark 3.

2 Combine the peppercorns and shallot with the breast meat, and season with a little salt. Use this mixture to stuff the boned legs. Put the onion, celery and carrot in an ovenproof dish with the tomato purée, stock and half the Madeira. Add the stuffed duck legs and bake in a moderate oven, at 160°C (325°F), Gas Mark 3, for 45 minutes.

3 Soak the raisins in the remaining Madeira. Remove the duck legs from the dish and keep hot. Add the raisins and Madeira to the sauce. Reduce to a glaze over a moderate heat. Whisk in the cream and reduce to a light coating consistency. Pour over the duck legs and serve.

KIG HA FARZ
BOILED MEATS WITH A FRUIT DUMPLING

SERVES 8

1.5 kg (3½ lb) chuck steak, trimmed and tied
750 g (1½ lb) pork belly, rinded and in one
piece
750 g (1½ lb) onions, peeled
100 g (4 oz) celery
250 g (9 oz) carrot
1 bouquet garni
salt and pepper
FARZ:
120 g (4½ oz) buckwheat flour
120 g (4½ oz) plain flour
6 tablespoons milk
6 tablespoons double cream
1 large egg
120 g (4½ oz) mixed dried fruit, including
prunes, raisins and sultanas
50 g (2 oz) sugar

1 Put the beef, pork, vegetables and bouquet garni in a large pan. Pour over enough water to cover by at least 7.5 cm (3 inches). Bring to the boil, season with salt and pepper and simmer for 2 hours.

2 Combine all the ingredients for the *farz* or dumpling together with a ladle of stock from the meats. They should form a slack dough. Wrap the *farz* in a double layer of foil to form a sausage. Seal both ends and poach for about 2 hours with the meats.

3 To serve, remove the meats from the pan and slice. Remove the *farz* from the foil and slice thickly. Remove the bouquet garni from the vegetables, and arrange the meat, *farz* and vegetables on a serving dish.

POTÉE BRETONNE
BEEF AND PORK HOTPOT

SERVES 10 TO 12

1.5 kg (3½ lb) shin of beef on the bone
750 g (1½ lb) belly of pork in one piece
750 g (1½ lb) smoked streaky bacon in one
piece
2.75 litres (5 pints) chicken stock
575 g (1¼ lb) onions, peeled and quartered
120 g (4½ oz) carrot, peeled and quartered
120 g (4½ oz) leek, sliced
1 large bouquet garni
1 clove
salt and pepper
TO GARNISH:
575 g (1¼ lb) pork sausages
575 g (1¼ lb) baby turnips, peeled and
quartered
575 g (1¼ lb) carrots, peeled and sliced
lengthways
575 g (1¼ lb) broad beans
2 small green cabbages
salt

1 Put the beef, pork and bacon in a very large saucepan. Pour over the stock and bring to the boil. Skim off any impurities. Add the vegetables, bouquet garni, clove and a little salt and pepper. Cover and simmer for 3 hours.

2 Remove the vegetables, bouquet garni and clove with a slotted spoon. Add the sausages, turnips and carrots. Simmer for 30 minutes. Add the broad beans and simmer for a further 30 minutes.

3 Separate the cabbage leaves. Blanch for 10 minutes in boiling salted water and drain. Form 12 small cabbage balls by wrapping the larger leaves around the inner ones, rolling into balls and squeezing out any excess moisture.

4 To serve, arrange the meats, sausages, turnips, carrots and broad beans in a large serving dish. Allow the cabbage balls to simmer in the stock for 2 or 3 minutes and add them to the serving dish. Serve the broth in a separate tureen.

POTÉE BRETONNE

BOULETTES BRETONNES *(ABOVE)*
PÂTÉ BRETON *(BELOW)*

PÂTÉ BRETON
BRETON PÂTÉ

Thinly sliced bacon fat could be used instead of caul fat in this recipe.

FOR A 1.2 LITRE (2 PINT) TERRINE
575 g (1¼ lb) lean belly of pork, minced
250 g (9 oz) smoked streaky bacon, minced
300 g (11 oz) fat pork, minced
2 teaspoons salt
2 teaspoons ground black pepper
4 juniper berries, crushed
1 tablespoon dried herbs
2 tablespoons Lambig, Calvados or brandy
2 eggs
caul fat, soaked in water
bay leaves, and pink peppercorns to garnish

1 Combine the meats, salt, half the pepper, juniper berries, dried herbs, spirit and eggs.

2 Line the terrine with caul fat. Fill it with the pâté mixture and lay one bay leaf on top. Fold the caul fat back over the pâté and sprinkle the rest of the pepper on top. Put the lid on the terrine and leave for at least 5 hours.

3 Stand the terrine in a tray of simmering water, which should come about halfway up the sides. Simmer over a low heat on top of the stove for 1½ to 2 hours. Cool and leave in the refrigerator for 24 hours before serving. Garnish with bay leaves and pink peppercorns.

BOULETTES BRETONNES
BRETON FAGGOTS

SERVES 8
caul fat
575 g (1¼ lb) lean belly of pork, minced
575 g (1¼ lb) green streaky bacon, minced
350 g (12 oz) fat pork, minced
1 teaspoon black pepper
½ nutmeg, grated
1 pinch of ground cloves
2 teaspoons mixed dried herbs
1 tablespoon chopped parsley

1 Soak the caul fat until white. Combine the meats, spices and herbs and divide into eight balls.

2 Wrap each *boulette* in caul fat and place in a roasting tin. Bake in a moderate oven, at 180°C (350°F), Gas Mark 4, for 45 minutes, basting once. Serve cold with French bread and pickles.

LARD NANTAIS
BRAISED PORK CHOPS AND LIVER

SERVES 4
caul fat to wrap the pork packages
4 × 100 g (4 oz) slices pig's liver
4 pork chops
200 g (7 oz) onion, carrot and celery, peeled and finely diced
2 cloves garlic, peeled and crushed
4 sage leaves
250 ml (8 fl oz) dry white wine
salt and pepper
40 g (1½ oz) butter

1 Soak the caul fat in a bowl of cold water. Gas Mark 6. Put four squares of caul on a work surface. Lay a slice of liver on top of each square and a chop on top of that. Wrap up the package.

2 Place the vegetables, garlic and sage on the bottom of an ovenproof dish. Lay the four meat packages on top. Pour over the wine and season with salt and pepper. Place a slice of butter on each package and bake in a moderately hot oven, at 200°C (400°F), Gas Mark 6, for 35 minutes, basting twice.

CÔTE DE BOEUF À LA PURÉE DE SARRASIN
ROAST RIB OF BEEF WITH BUCKWHEAT PURÉE

SERVES 4
1.25 kg (2½ lb) rib of beef
salt and pepper
BUCKWHEAT PURÉE:
100 g (4 oz) buckwheat flour
400 ml (14 fl oz) water
575 g (1¼ lb) potatoes, peeled and roughly chopped
salt and pepper
65 g (2½ oz) butter
1 egg

1 Rub the beef all over with freshly ground black pepper and sprinkle with a little salt. Preheat the oven to 220°C (425°F), Gas Mark 7. Roast for 30 minutes for rare, 50 minutes for medium and 60 minutes for well done.

2 Meanwhile, combine the buckwheat flour and water in a pan. Bring to the boil, stirring continuously, and simmer until the mixture becomes a thick porridge.

3 Cook the potatoes in salted water. Drain and mash. Combine the buckwheat porridge and mashed potato. Beat in the butter and then the egg. Check the seasoning, adding plenty of pepper. If you prefer it completely smooth, sieve the purée.

4 Allow the beef to rest for 10 minutes before carving. Serve with the buckwheat purée.

POULET SAUTÉ À LA NAZAIRIENNE
CHICKEN SAUTÉED WITH TOMATO AND TARRAGON SAUCE

SERVES 4
1 chicken weighing 1.5-1.75 kg (3½-4 lb)
salt and pepper
15 g (½ oz) butter or chicken fat
1 shallot, peeled and finely diced
1 clove garlic, peeled and crushed
100 ml (3½ fl oz) Muscadet
300 ml (½ pint) chicken stock
2 beef tomatoes, peeled, seeded and roughly chopped
3 branches of tarragon or 1 teaspoon dried tarragon
300 ml (½ pint) double cream
2 tablespoons chopped parsley and fresh tarragon

1 Cut the chicken into eight joints (drumsticks, thighs, wings with breast attached and breast pieces) or ask your butcher to do this for you. Season lightly with salt and pepper.

2 Melt the fat in a large sauté pan. Sauté the chicken pieces, skin side down, for 5 minutes. Turn the pieces and sauté for another 10 minutes.

3 Add the shallot and garlic and fry briefly. Remove the chicken pieces and drain off the fat in the pan. Deglaze with the wine and bring to the boil. Return the chicken pieces to the pan and add the stock, tomatoes and tarragon. Cook for 20 minutes longer.

4 Arrange the chicken pieces in a serving dish and keep hot. Reduce the liquid in the pan. Add the cream and heat rapidly. Strain the sauce into a clean pan. Adjust the seasoning and stir in the chopped herbs. Coat the chicken with the sauce and serve.

CÔTE DE BOEUF À LA PURÉE DE SARRASIN

LAPIN SAUTÉ AU CIDRE

LAPIN SAUTÉ AU CIDRE
RABBIT SAUTÉED WITH CIDER

SERVES 4
50 g (2 oz) butter
1 rabbit weighing about 1 kg (2 lb), cut into pieces
120 g (4½ oz) green streaky bacon, diced
400 g (14 oz) onion, peeled and sliced
40 g (1½ oz) plain flour
750 ml (1¼ pints) dry cider
2 sprigs thyme
2 sprigs tarragon
salt and pepper
120 g (4½ oz) mushrooms, sliced

1 Heat the butter in a frying pan and fry the pieces of rabbit until well coloured. Transfer the rabbit to a large casserole.

2 Fry the bacon and onion until golden brown and sprinkle with flour. Allow to cook for 2 minutes, then pour over 250 ml (8 fl oz) cider and bring to the boil, stirring so as to prevent any lumps.

3 Transfer the onion, bacon and sauce to the casserole with the rabbit. Add the remaining cider, thyme and tarragon, and season with salt and pepper. Simmer for 40 minutes, then add the mushrooms and simmer for another 15 minutes.

LAPIN À LA GELÉE DE MUSCADET
RABBIT IN MUSCADET JELLY WITH HERBS

SERVES 4
saddle and hind legs of a rabbit (they should weigh about 575 g/1¼ lb)
100 ml (3½ fl oz) Muscadet
1 tablespoon finely diced shallot
1 tablespoon chopped parsley
2 teaspoons chopped rosemary
2 teaspoons chopped thyme
½ clove garlic, peeled and crushed
pepper
250 ml (8 fl oz) chicken stock
2 leaves gelatine (or 2 teaspoons)
4 slices green streaky bacon

1 Cut the saddle and legs into eight pieces – four leg and four saddle (you may bone the saddle). Marinate overnight in wine, shallots, herbs, garlic and pepper.

2 Heat the chicken stock slightly. Soak the gelatine in water, then dissolve in the stock.

3 Line an ovenproof dish with bacon slices. Arrange the rabbit on top. Combine the stock with the marinade and pour over the rabbit. Cover with foil and bake in a cool oven, at 150°C (300°F), Gas Mark 2, for 2 hours.

4 Leave overnight, then turn out and serve with a salad and crusty bread.

POULET RÔTI À LA CORSAIRE
ROAST CHICKEN CORSAIR-STYLE

SERVES 4
1 roasting chicken weighing 1.5-1.75 kg (3½-4 lb)
salt and pepper
25 g (1 oz) butter, melted
STUFFING:
25 g (1 oz) onion, peeled and diced
15 g (½ oz) butter
250 g (9 oz) pork, minced
7 tablespoons fresh breadcrumbs
1 red chilli, diced
3 prunes, chopped
1 tablespoon raisins
1 pinch each of cinnamon, allspice, coriander, mace and clove
salt

1 Season the inside of the chicken with salt and pepper.

2 Fry the onion gently in butter until transparent. Combine with the other stuffing ingredients. Stuff the inside of the chicken with this mixture.

3 Brush the chicken with melted butter. Stand on a rack over a roasting tin. Roast in a moderately hot oven, at 190°C (375°F), Gas Mark 5, for 1¼-1½ hours.

VEGETABLE DISHES

Rich soil and a favourable climate provide Brittany with an abundance of vegetables. Combined with other regional specialities like cider and fish, these are then used to create dishes like *Artichauts à la Bretonne* or *Tomates Farcies à la Morue*. For summer, there are salads like *Salade à la Peau de Canard*, which combines salad leaves with crispy fried duck skin; for the winter, there is *Haricots à la Creme* or *Bardatte*, in which cabbage leaves are filled with a minced rabbit stuffing.

ARTICHAUTS FARCIS
STUFFED ARTICHOKES

SERVES 4
5 large artichokes
salt and pepper
1 tablespoon lemon juice
20 g (¾ oz) butter
200 g (7 oz) lean bacon, diced
200 g (7 oz) onion, peeled and finely diced
4 cloves garlic, peeled and finely diced
1 pinch of thyme
200 g (7 oz) cooked chicken breast, diced
2 tablespoons chopped parsley
oil

1 Break the stalks off the artichokes and pull away any tough outer leaves. Trim off about 2 cm (¾ inch) from the tops of the leaves on 4 artichokes. Cook all the artichokes in boiling salted water acidulated with lemon juice for 25 minutes.

2 Drain the artichokes and cool. Leaving the three outer rows of leaves intact on the trimmed artichokes, remove the inner leaves and the furry chokes. Discard all the leaves and the choke on the fifth artichoke and dice the heart.

3 Melt the butter in a pan. Sauté the bacon and onion until they start to colour. Add the garlic and thyme and cook for 1 minute longer. Stir in the diced chicken, parsley and diced artichoke heart. Season with salt and pepper. Spoon the filling into the four prepared artichokes.

4 Brush with oil, wrap in foil and bake in a moderately hot oven, at 200°C (400°F), Gas Mark 6, for 20 minutes. To serve, unwrap them and arrange on a dish.

ARTICHAUTS À LA BRETONNE
ARTICHOKE HEARTS BRAISED IN CIDER

SERVES 4
8 small artichokes (or 4 very large ones)
1 tablespoon lemon juice
90 g (3½ oz) butter
200 g (7 oz) onion, peeled and diced
400 ml (14 fl oz) sweet cider
salt and pepper
2 tablespoons chopped herbs, including parsley, chives and chervil

1 Break the stems off the artichokes. Pare away all the leaves, leaving only the hearts and the furry chokes. Cut out the chokes with a sharp knife. Blanch the hearts for 5 minutes in boiling water and lemon juice. Drain and cut into quarters.

2 Melt 50 g (2 oz) butter in a large sauté pan. Add the onion and fry gently until transparent. Add the artichoke hearts and pour over the cider. Braise for 20 minutes.

3 Lift out the artichoke hearts and keep warm on a serving dish. Reduce the liquid to a glaze and adjust the seasoning. Beat in the rest of the butter. Pour the sauce over the artichoke hearts and garnish with the herbs.

ARTICHAUTS À LA BRETONNE

SALADE À LA PEAU DE CANARD *(ABOVE)*
BEIGNETS DE CHOU-FLEUR *(BELOW)*

BEIGNETS DE CHOU-FLEUR
CAULIFLOWER FRITTERS

SERVES 4
250 g (9 oz) cauliflower
1 egg, separated
120 g (4½ oz) plain flour
100 ml (3½ fl oz) water
3 tablespoons oil
oil for deep frying
salt

1 Separate the cauliflower into small florets.

2 Beat the egg yolk into the flour, then whisk in the water to form a stiff batter. Beat in the oil.

3 Preheat the frying oil. Whisk the egg white until it forms stiff peaks and fold into the batter.

4 Dip the cauliflower in batter and deep fry in the hot oil for 5 to 7 minutes until golden. Drain on absorbent paper and sprinkle with salt.

SALADE DE HARICOTS BLANCS AU CERFEUIL
BEAN AND CHERVIL SALAD

SERVES 4
2 teaspoons Dijon mustard
1 pinch of sea salt
2 tablespoons sherry vinegar
4 tablespoons groundnut oil
4 tablespoons walnut oil
300 g (11 oz) cooked haricot beans
freshly ground black pepper
1-2 tablespoons chopped chervil, to garnish

1 Put the mustard in a bowl with the salt. Whisk in the sherry vinegar. Then whisk in the oils, a little at a time, so that the dressing thickens slightly.

2 Toss the beans in the dressing. Add plenty of black pepper and garnish liberally with chervil.

SALADE À LA PEAU DE CANARD
SALAD WITH CRISP DUCK SKINS

SERVES 4
150 g (5 oz) duck skin, from neck, breast and carcass
1 slice bread
1 clove garlic, peeled
mixed salad greens (corn salad or endive, chicory, young dandelions)
1 tablespoon sherry vinegar
salt and pepper

1 Cut the duck skin into pieces the size of a postage stamp. Place the skin in a frying pan and cook over a moderately low heat for about 20 minutes, allowing it to colour and slowly render its fat.

2 When the skin has just begun to colour, strain some of the fat into a fresh pan and fry the bread until golden. Rub with garlic and cut into small cubes.

3 Arrange the salad greens in a bowl. Pour over the vinegar and season with salt and pepper. Toss lightly and add the croûtons. As soon as the duck skin is crisp, add to the salad with some of the remaining fat. Toss the salad again and serve at once.

POMMES AU FOUR À LA CAILLEBOTTE
JACKET POTATOES WITH SOFT CHEESE AND CHIVES

Caillebotte is a fresh cheese made by draining unpasteurized sour milk – cow's or goat's – over muslin. You can buy freshly made curd cheese from wholefood shops.

SERVES 4
4 large potatoes, each weighing about
300 g (11 oz)
salt
200 g (7 oz) freshly prepared curd cheese
2 tablespoons chopped chives

1 Wash the potatoes, dry and rub the skins with salt. Wrap the potatoes in foil and bake in a moderately hot oven at 200°C (400°F), Gas Mark 6, for 1¼ hours.

2 Split open the potatoes by scoring the tops with a cross. Fluff up the insides with a fork. Put a large spoonful of curd cheese on top and garnish with chopped chives.

POMMES À LA BIGOUDEN
BAKED SLICED POTATOES

SERVES 4
65 g (2½ oz) butter, melted
575 g (1¼ lb) waxy potatoes
salt and pepper

1 Brush a shallow oven-proof dish with a little of the butter. Slice the potatoes, without peeling them, about 3 mm (⅛ inch) thick. Season with salt and pepper and coat in the remaining butter.

2 Lay the potato slices overlapping in the dish. They should not be more than two layers deep. Bake in a moderately hot oven, at 200°C (400°F), Gas Mark 6, for 45 minutes or until golden brown.

TOMATES FARCIES À LA MORUE
TOMATOES STUFFED WITH SALT COD PURÉE

SERVES 4
575 g (1¼ lb) salt cod
150 ml (¼ pint) olive oil
juice of ½ lemon
2 tablespoons double cream
salt and pepper
4 beef tomatoes

1 Lay the cod on a rack standing in a large bowl or basin. Cover with plenty of water, changing the water often over the next 48 hours to remove the salt. Remove the skin.

2 Poach the cod for 8 minutes in a pan of simmering water. Drain and discard all the bones. Pound the flaked cod in a mortar until thoroughly mashed. Incorporate the oil a little at a time, still pounding so that you obtain a creamy consistency. Stir in the lemon juice, cream, salt and pepper.

3 Cut off the tops of the tomatoes and carefully scoop out the insides. Fill the empty tomato cases with the cod purée and replace the tops. Place the tomatoes on a baking sheet and bake in a moderately hot oven, at 200°C (400°F), Gas Mark 6, for 15 to 20 minutes. Serve piping hot.

CHOU-FLEUR EN BALLON *(ABOVE, RECIPE PAGE 63)*
POMMES À LA BIGOUDENN *(BELOW)*

HARICOTS À LA CRÈME

CHOU-FLEUR EN BALLON
CAULIFLOWER WITH HAM AND TOMATO

SERVES 4

1 cauliflower weighing about 350-450 g
(12 oz-1 lb), quartered
salt and pepper
25 g (1 oz) butter
1 shallot, peeled and finely diced
1 clove garlic, peeled and crushed
50 g (2 oz) streaky bacon, diced
1 teaspoon sugar
250 g (9 oz) tomatoes, chopped
1 large slice ham
1 tablespoon finely chopped parsley to garnish

1 Cook the cauliflower for 15 to 20 minutes in boiling salted water.

2 Meanwhile, melt the butter in a pan and fry the shallot gently until soft. Add the garlic and bacon and, when the bacon starts to colour, sprinkle the sugar over it. Add the tomatoes and cook over a moderate heat for 20 to 30 minutes. Adjust the seasoning.

3 Cut the slice of ham into four. Reassemble the cauliflower in a bowl of similar size and slip a piece of ham between each of the segments. Pour over the tomato sauce and garnish with chopped parsley.

HARICOTS À LA CRÈME
HARICOT BEANS WITH BACON AND CREAM

SERVES 4

200 g (7 oz) dried haricot beans, soaked overnight
3 rashers smoked streaky bacon
25 g (1 oz) butter
150 ml (¼ pint) chicken stock
100 ml (3½ fl oz) double cream
1 teaspoon savory
salt and pepper
1 tablespoon chopped parsley

1 Put the beans in a pan with water to cover. Bring to the boil, simmer for 10 minutes and drain. Transfer to a fresh pan of water and simmer for about 2 hours. Drain.

2 Cut the rind off the bacon and slice finely across the grain. Sauté these thin *lardons* in butter until they start to become crisp. Deglaze the pan with chicken stock and reduce to a glaze. Add the beans and coat in the glaze. Pour over the cream and stir in the savory. Bring back to the boil and reduce until the cream thickens. Season with salt only if you feel it is absolutely necessary and plenty of pepper. Garnish with chopped parsley.

BARDATTE
CABBAGE LEAVES STUFFED WITH MINCED RABBIT

SERVES 4

250 g (9 oz) green cabbage leaves
25 g (1 oz) butter
75 g (3 oz) onions, peeled and diced
65 g (2½ oz) mushrooms, chopped
50 g (2 oz) fresh breadcrumbs
150 ml (¼ pint) milk
1 small egg, lightly beaten
250 g (9 oz) minced rabbit
1 tablespoon fresh thyme leaves
salt and pepper
strips of pork fat (optional)
300 ml (½ pint) dry white wine
300 ml (½ pint) chicken stock

1 Separate the cabbage leaves and blanch for 4 minutes in boiling water. Drain and allow to cool.

2 Melt the butter in a pan and sweat the onions and mushrooms. Soak the breadcrumbs in milk and squeeze out excess milk. Combine the onions, mushrooms, breadcrumbs, egg, rabbit, thyme, salt and pepper.

3 Form balls of minced rabbit stuffing weighing about 50 g (2 oz) each. Wrap in cabbage leaves, and pork fat if using, and fasten the packages with kitchen string.

4 Place in an ovenproof dish with wine and stock. Cover and braise for 1½ hours, either on top of the stove or in a moderate oven at 180°C (350°F), Gas Mark 4. Baste from time to time. To serve, remove the string.

PANCAKES

Brittany is renowned for its pancakes, and justly so, for these must be one of the most versatile of all French dishes. The buckwheat *galettes*, for example, can be filled with tuna or ham for a simple supper or, dressed up with seafood and cream, can provide the most elegant hors-d'oeuvre. *Crêpes dentelles* can be savoury or sweet – but are perhaps at their most delicious when filled with a strawberry cream, in *Crêpes Fourrées aux Fraises*.

CRÊPES DENTELLES
BASIC PANCAKE RECIPE

MAKES 16 TO 20×15 CM (6 INCH) CRÊPES
120 g (4½ oz) plain flour
3 eggs
250 ml (8 fl oz) milk
3 tablespoons melted butter
butter or oil for greasing the pan

1 Sift the flour into a bowl. Beat in the eggs one at a time. Beat in the milk until you obtain a smooth batter, then whisk in the butter. Leave to stand for 2 hours.

2 Heat a 15 cm (6 inch) frying pan and brush with butter or oil. When it sizzles, pour in 2 to 3 tablespoons of batter and shake the pan so that the batter spreads evenly. Fry until the bottom is lightly coloured, toss or turn with a spatula and continue frying for another 20 seconds or so to cook the other side. Turn on to a dish. Make the other pancakes in the same way.

GALETTES DE SARRASIN
BUCKWHEAT PANCAKES

MAKES 8 × 20 CM (8 INCH) or 4 TO 5×30 CM (12 INCH) PANCAKES
100 g (4 oz) buckwheat flour
25 g (1 oz) plain flour
3 eggs
300 ml (½ pint) skimmed milk
3 tablespoons melted butter
butter or oil for greasing the pan

1 Sift both flours into a bowl. Beat in the eggs one at a time. Beat in the milk until you obtain a smooth batter. Allow to rest for at least 2 hours.

2 Just before frying the *galettes*, stir in the melted butter. Heat a large frying pan or griddle and brush with butter or oil. Pour a little batter on to the pan or griddle and spread it evenly (in Brittany they do this with a wooden rake, called a *raclette*). When one side is lightly coloured, turn and cook the other side. Cook all the pancakes in this way.

GALETTES AU JAMBON DE PAYS
BUCKWHEAT PANCAKES WITH AIR-CURED HAM

SERVES 4
4 large buckwheat pancakes (see previous recipe)
25 g (1 oz) butter
25 g (1 oz) shallots, peeled and finely diced
120 g (4½ oz) mushrooms, sliced
1 tablespoon dry cider
120 ml (4 fl oz) double cream
salt and pepper
4 slices *jambon de campagne* (or *prosciutto*)

1 Prepare the pancakes and keep them hot. Melt the butter in a frying pan, add the shallots and sauté until transparent. Add the mushrooms and sauté. Deglaze the pan with cider. Pour over the cream, reduce to a coating consistency, and season.

2 Lay a slice of ham on each pancake. Spoon over some mushrooms and cream. Fold each pancake into four and serve.

GALETTES AU JAMBON DE PAYS

GALETTES AU THON

GALETTES AU THON
TUNA PANCAKES

SERVES 4
15 g (½ oz) butter
50 g (2 oz) shallots, peeled and finely diced
1 × 120 g (4½ oz) can tuna
120 ml (4 fl oz) double cream
1 teaspoon lemon juice
salt and pepper
4 large buckwheat pancakes (page 64)

1 Melt the butter in a pan. Add the shallots and fry gently until transparent. Cool slightly and add to the tuna. Whip the cream until it holds its shape on the whisk. Season the tuna with lemon juice, salt and pepper and fold in the cream.

2 Spread some tuna mousse over each *galette* and fold into four.

GALETTES AUX FONDS D'ARTICHAUTS
ARTICHOKE PANCAKES

SERVES 4
4 large buckwheat pancakes (page 64)
4 turned artichoke hearts
1.25 litres (2¼ pints) water
2 tablespoons lemon juice
20 g (¾ oz) butter
25 g (1 oz) shallots, peeled and finely diced
1½ tablespoons Muscadet
120 ml (4 fl oz) double cream
1 teaspoon wholegrain mustard
salt and pepper

1 Prepare the pancakes and keep hot. Blanch the artichoke hearts for 5 minutes in a pan of boiling water acidulated with 1 tablespoon lemon juice. Lift out the hearts with a slotted spoon and drain well. Boil 500 ml (18 fl oz) of the cooking liquid and reduce by half.

2 Melt the butter in a pan and sweat the shallots until transparent. Add the reduced cooking liquid from the artichokes, wine, cream, mustard and the remaining tablespoon lemon juice. Add the sliced artichoke hearts. Cook over a moderate heat for 15 minutes until the artichoke hearts become tender and the sauce reduces to a light coating consistency. Season with salt and pepper.

3 Spread the filling over the pancakes, fold and serve piping hot.

Note: to turn an artichoke, break off the stem, pulling out the fibres that go into the artichoke. Pare away the leaves with a sharp knife leaving only the yellowish bottom and the furry choke. This must then be pulled out after blanching.

GALETTES AUX OEUFS ET AU FROMAGE
CHEESE AND EGG PANCAKES

SERVES 4
300 ml (½ pint) buckwheat pancake batter (page 64)
butter or oil for greasing the pan
65 g (2½ oz) butter, melted
4 small eggs
8 tablespoons grated cheese

1 Heat and grease a griddle or a 30 cm (12 inch) frying pan. Pour some of the batter on to the pan or griddle. Spread it in a thin even layer. When one side is lightly coloured, turn it over to cook the other side.

2 Brush the *galette* with melted butter and break 1 egg on to it slightly off-centre. Spread the white over the pancake so that it cooks quickly. Sprinkle 2 tablespoons of grated cheese over the pancake. As soon as the egg is cooked and the cheese melting, fold the *galette* into four. Brush with more melted butter and serve. Repeat this stage to make another three pancakes.

CRÊPES FOURRÉES AUX FRAISES
STRAWBERRY PANCAKES

SERVES 4
8 crêpes dentelles (page 64)
575 g (1¼ lb) strawberries
225 g (8 oz) caster sugar
juice of ½ lemon
120 ml (4 fl oz) double cream

1 Keep the pancakes hot. Mash the strawberries, reserving 8 small berries for the decoration. Combine the crushed strawberries with 200 g (7 oz) sugar and lemon juice.

2 Whip the cream with the remaining sugar until firm. Fill the pancakes with the mashed strawberries and roll up.

3 Decorate the tops of the pancakes with piped cream and the reserved strawberries.

CRÊPES AUX POMMES
APPLE PANCAKES

MAKES 8 × 20 CM (8 INCH) PANCAKES
75 g (3 oz) butter
4 small eating apples, peeled, cored and sliced
half quantity basic pancake batter (page 64)
2 tablespoons icing sugar

1 For each apple pancake, melt a knob of butter in a 20 cm (8 inch) frying pan. Arrange half a sliced apple in the pan. Fry on one side until soft and golden, then turn over and fry on the other side.

2 Pour enough pancake batter into the pan to cover the bottom. Cook one side and turn carefully. While the second side is cooking, sprinkle a little icing sugar over the pancake. Slip it on to a dessert plate and glaze under a hot grill for a few seconds. Repeat with the rest of the apples and pancake batter.

CRÊPES AUX MARRONS
CHESTNUT PANCAKES

SERVES 4
12 crêpes dentelles (page 64)
65 g (2½ oz) liquid honey
120 g (4½ oz) chestnut purée
85 ml (3 fl oz) double cream
2 tablespoons rum (optional)

1 Keep the pancakes hot until required or reheat at the last moment.

2 Warm the honey very slightly in a small saucepan. Beat it into the chestnut purée until you obtain a smooth consistency. Whip the double cream until stiff, and fold into the chestnut and honey purée. Add the rum at this stage if you are using it. Fill a piping bag with a plain 1 cm (½ inch) tube with the chestnut purée.

3 Pipe a band of purée down the centre of each pancake and roll it up like a cigar. Serve at once.

CRÊPES FLAMBÉES AU LAMBIG
PANCAKES FLAMED IN LAMBIG

SERVES 6
basic pancake batter (page 64)
6 eating apples, peeled, cored and diced
65 g (2½ oz) butter
120 g (4½ oz) caster sugar
6 tablespoons Lambig (or Calvados)

1 Make 18 pancakes and keep hot while you prepare the filling.

2 Place the apple in a pan with the butter and 80 g (3 oz) sugar. Cook over a gentle heat until tender and golden brown.

3 Spoon a little apple on to the pancakes and roll them up. Arrange neatly in a pan and keep hot.

4 Put the remaining sugar in a pan with the Lambig (or Calvados). Stir to dissolve the sugar. Heat gently and flame the spirit. Pour over the pancakes and serve.

CRÊPES FOURRÉES AUX FRAISES *(ABOVE)*
CRÊPES AUX POMMES *(BELOW)*

DESSERTS

Breton desserts have all the beautiful simplicity of real country cooking, made, as they are, from produce from the farm or garden. Cream, butter and eggs play a large part, with apples and strawberries among the favourite fruits. There are custards like *Crème Sainte Anne*, fresh cream cheeses, apple fritters and turnovers like *Choquarts*, and batter puddings. There is also a Breton tradition of baking, to be found in cakes like the butter-rich *Kuign-Aman* and biscuits like the dainty, almond-flavoured *Bigoudens* or melt-in-the-mouth *Craquelins*.

GÂTEAU BRETON
BRETON CAKE

SERVES 8
200 g (7 oz) caster sugar
4 egg yolks
250 g (9 oz) butter, softened
3 tablespoons Calvados (optional)
300 g (11 oz) plain unbleached flour
1 egg, separated

1 Cream the sugar and egg yolks. Add the butter and continue the creaming process. This will take 15 minutes with an electric whisk or longer by hand. Beat in the Calvados if you are using it and finally beat in the flour.

2 Grease a 20 cm (8 inch) baking tin. Fill the tin with the cake mixture and spread it evenly. Beat the egg white and brush over the cake surface. Repeat, using the yolk. Score the surface with a sharp-pronged fork, making a wavy pattern.

3 Bake the cake in a moderately hot oven, at 190°C (375°F), Gas Mark 5, for 35 minutes. If you have used Calvados, you may need to bake the cake for a little longer. Turn out and allow to cool on a wire rack. Serve cold.

CRÉMETS AU COULIS DE FRAISES
HEART-SHAPED CHEESES WITH STRAWBERRY SAUCE

SERVES 4
250 ml (8 fl oz) double cream
1 egg white
100 g (4 oz) *fromage blanc*
250 g (9 oz) strawberries
1 tablespoon lemon juice
2 tablespoons caster sugar

1 Line four *coeur à la crème* moulds with muslin. Whip the double cream and beat the egg white separately until stiff. Beat the *fromage blanc* with a spoon and fold into the whipped cream. Fold in the beaten egg white. Spoon the mixture into the moulds and turn over the muslin to cover the *crémets*. Leave to chill for 3 hours.

2 Liquidize the strawberries, reserving 4 berries for the decoration, with the lemon juice and caster sugar.

3 Turn out the heart-shaped cheeses on to four plates. Surround with strawberry sauce and decorate the *crémets* with slices of strawberry.

CRÉMETS AU COULIS DE FRAISES

KUIGN-AMAN *(ABOVE)*
FAR BRETON *(BELOW)*

KUIGN-AMAN
BRETON BUTTER CAKE

SERVES 12
450 ml (¾ pint) water
15 g (½ oz) fresh yeast or 1 teaspoon dried yeast
750 g (1½ lb) strong white flour
1 teaspoon salt
575 g (1¼ lb) butter
575 g (1¼ lb) granulated sugar
1 egg, beaten

1 Heat the water to 38°C (100°F) and dissolve the yeast in it. Sift the flour and salt into a large bowl and add the water. Knead for at least 10 minutes. Cover the dough and leave in a warm place to double in size.

2 Knock back the dough and roll out on a floured board. Cover half the surface with butter, leaving a gap of 2.5 cm (1 inch) around the edge. Sprinkle the butter with 450 g (1 lb) sugar. Fold over the dough to enclose the butter and sugar, and seal the edges. Allow to rest for 15 minutes. Roll out to about 2.5 cm (1 inch) thick and fold again. Repeat three times, resting the dough between each rolling.

3 Roll out the dough to form a circle about 30 cm (12 inches) in diameter and lay on a greased baking sheet. Brush the top with beaten egg and sprinkle with the remaining sugar. Score a crisscross pattern over the surface. Bake in a moderately hot oven, at 200°C (400°F), Gas Mark 6, for 30 minutes.

FAR BRETON
BRETON BATTER PUDDING

SERVES 6 TO 8
200 g (7 oz) stoned prunes
350 ml (12 fl oz) boiling China tea
120 ml (4 fl oz) rum
100 g (4 oz) plain flour
4 eggs
100 g (4 oz) caster sugar
750 ml (1¼ pints) milk

1 Soak the prunes in tea and 4 tablespoons of rum until well swollen. This may take anything from 3 to 12 hours, depending on quality and type.

2 Sift the flour into a large bowl. Beat in the eggs one at a time and add the sugar, milk and remaining rum. Beat for 5 minutes.

3 Butter a round 25 cm (10 inch) flan dish or cake tin. Pour in the batter and add the drained prunes. Bake in a moderately hot oven, at 190°C (375°F), Gas Mark 5, for about 40 minutes. Look at the pudding after 30 minutes and, if it has become very dark already, cover with foil.

4 This pudding is usually served cold but is also delicious hot, straight from the oven.

BEIGNETS AU CIDRE
APPLE AND CIDER FRITTERS

SERVES 4
175 g (6 oz) self-raising flour
1 egg
250 ml (8 fl oz) medium cider
1 tablespoon Lambig (or Calvados)
4 cooking apples, peeled and cored
200 ml (⅓ pint) sunflower oil
50 g (2 oz) butter
100 g (4 oz) caster sugar

1 Sift the flour twice. Beat the egg with 2 tablespoons of cider and stir into the flour. Beat in the rest of the cider, a little at a time, taking care that no lumps form. Stir in the Lambig. Cut each apple into six segments.

2 Heat the oil and butter in a large pan. Dip a few pieces of apple in the batter and fry until golden on both sides. Drain on absorbent paper and sprinkle with caster sugar.

CHOQUARTS
SPICED APPLE TURNOVERS

SERVES 4
575 g (1¼ lb) cooking apples, peeled, cored and
chopped
120 g (4½ oz) soft brown sugar
1 teaspoon powdered cinnamon
1 tablespoon raisins
400 g (14 oz) puff pastry
1 egg yolk

1 Cook the apples, sugar, cinnamon and raisins in a little water until the mixture forms a compôte. Allow to cool.

2 Roll out the pastry and cut out four 15 cm (6 inch) circles. Brush the edges with water. Spoon the cold apple into the middle of each circle. Fold and seal the edges of the pastry, enclosing the apple, and crimp the edges neatly. Brush the tops with lightly beaten egg yolk and decorate with the point of a sharp knife. Lay the *choquarts* on a prepared baking sheet and bake in a hot oven, at 230°C (450°F), Gas Mark 8, for 20 minutes. Serve hot or cold.

CRAQUELINS
BRETON BISCUITS

MAKES 25 TO 30
250 g (9 oz) plain flour
150 g (5 oz) butter
25 g (1 oz) caster sugar
salt
3 egg yolks
1 tablespoon milk
icing sugar (optional)

1 Rub the flour and butter together until they form crumbs. Add the sugar and a small pinch of salt. Combine 2 egg yolks with milk, add to the flour and work into a smooth paste. Allow to rest for 20 minutes.

2 Roll out the paste to 3 mm (⅛ inch) thick and cut into 5 cm (2 inch) squares. Combine the remaining egg yolk with a teaspoon of water. Brush the biscuits with beaten egg yolk and score the surface with a sharp-pronged fork. Lay the biscuits on baking sheets and bake in a hot oven, at 230°C (450°F), Gas Mark 8, for about 8 minutes.

3 Transfer to a wire tray to cool and, if liked, dust with icing sugar.

BIGOUDENS
BRETON ALMOND BISCUITS

MAKES ABOUT 35
300 g (11 oz) plain flour
½ teaspoon baking powder
100 g (4 oz) butter, softened
150 g (5 oz) caster sugar
3 egg yolks
2 tablespoons single cream
1 tablespoon Cognac
120 g (4½ oz) almonds, roughly chopped

1 Sift the flour and baking powder on to a work surface. Make a hollow in the centre and add the butter, sugar, 2 egg yolks, cream and Cognac. Carefully work these ingredients into the flour and finally incorporate the almonds. Roll into a ball and allow to rest for 20 minutes.

2 Roll out the paste on a floured work surface until 5 mm (¼ inch) thick. Cut into circles, triangles, rectangles and crescent-shaped pieces. Brush the tops with beaten egg yolk and lay the biscuits on baking sheets covered with silicone paper or with greased greaseproof paper. Bake in a moderately hot oven, at 200°C (400°F), Gas Mark 6, for 15 minutes until crisp. Lay the *bigoudens* on wire trays to cool.

BIGOUDENS *(ABOVE)*
CHOQUARTS *(BELOW)*

GÂTEAU AUX MARRONS *(ABOVE)*
SALADE DE FRAISES À L'ÉCORCE D'ORANGE *(BELOW)*

CRÈME SAINTE ANNE
ST ANNE CREAM

SERVES 4
120 g (4½ oz) caster sugar
15 g (½ oz) unsalted butter
50 g (2 oz) macaroons, roughly chopped
300 ml (½ pint) milk
1 egg and 3 egg yolks

1 Put 65 g (2½ oz) sugar in a pan and moisten with 2 tablespoons water. Bring to the boil and cook to a mid-amber caramel. Pour the caramel into four ramekins and allow to set. Place a thin slice of butter on the caramel and sprinkle with chopped macaroons.

2 Heat the milk to simmering point. Whisk the egg, egg yolks and remaining sugar until creamy. Beat in the hot milk and pour into the prepared ramekins.

3 Stand the ramekins in a tray of simmering water which comes halfway up their sides. Bake in a moderate oven, at 160°C (325°F), Gas mark 3, for 20 to 25 minutes until set. Allow to cool and turn out.

GÂTEAU AUX MARRONS
CHESTNUT GÂTEAU

SERVES 8
7 eggs
200 g (7 oz) caster sugar
200 g (7 oz) plain flour
100 g (4 oz) butter, melted
FILLING:
200 g (7 oz) chestnut purée
1 tablespoon brown rum
100 g (4 oz) caster sugar
300 ml (½ pint) double cream
TOPPING:
100 g (4 oz) dark chocolate
250 ml (8 fl oz) water
400 g (14 oz) granulated sugar
8 marrons glacés (optional)

1 Whisk the eggs and sugar until they triple their volume and become firm. Fold in the flour and butter, alternating them. Pour the sponge mixture into a 20 cm (8 inch) sponge tin and bake in a moderate oven, at 180°C (350°F), Gas Mark 4, for 35 minutes. Turn out and allow to cool.

2 Combine the chestnut purée, rum and sugar. Whip the cream until stiff and fold into the purée. Cut the cake into three and spread the filling on the two middle pieces. Re-assemble the sponge.

3 Melt the chocolate over a very low heat with 1 tablespoon of water. Add the rest of the water and the sugar. Boil to 110°C (225°F). Allow to cool slightly without stirring. Coat the gâteau in the chocolate glaze. If you like, decorate with marrons glacés.

SALADE DE FRAISES À L'ÉCORCE D'ORANGE
STRAWBERRY SALAD WITH CANDIED ORANGE PEEL

SERVES 4
zest and juice of 1 orange
120 g (4½ oz) granulated sugar
120 ml (4 fl oz) water
juice of ½ lemon
575 g (1¼ lb) strawberries

1 Cut the orange zest in 5 cm (2 inch) strips. Dissolve the sugar in the water and bring to the boil. Add the orange zest and simmer over a very low heat for 2 hours. Lift out the orange zest and allow to drain on a wire tray.

2 Add the orange and lemon juice to the sugar syrup and allow to cool. Put the strawberries in a bowl and spoon over the syrup. Leave to macerate for 30 minutes in the refrigerator. Decorate with the candied orange zest and serve.

INDEX